S.O.S. Stand to!

Sergeant Reginald Grant

Patching up the "Pipped"

S.O.S.

STAND TO!

BY

SERGEANT REGINALD GRANT

1ST FIELD ARTILLERY BRIGADE, 1ST CANADIAN DIVISION

ILLUSTRATED

1918

DEDICATION

IN HUMBLE, REVERENT SPIRIT I DEDICATE THESE PAGES TO THE MEMORY OF THE LADS WHO SERVED WITH ME IN THE "SACRIFICE BATTERY," AND WHO GAVE THEIR LIVES THAT THOSE BEHIND MIGHT LIVE, AND, ALSO, IN BROTHERLY AFFECTION AND ESTEEM TO MY BROTHERS, GORDON AND BILLY, WHO ARE STILL FIGHTING THE GOOD FIGHT AND KEEPING THE FAITH.

REMARK PREFATORY

The general purpose and scope of the rehearsal of my three years' personal experience while in the artillery arm of the First Division of Canada's overseas forces is to lay before the reader an outline of the movement of our Division as it may be gathered from the performance of my own specific duties, with especial reference to the battles of Ypres (the 2nd), Givenchy, Sanctuary Woods (Ypres 3rd), the Somme and Vimy Ridge.

Very little attention or space has been devoted to the detail of initiatory camp life, drill, rations and the like; even had I the space to do so, those features have been liberally covered by a number of earlier writers; besides, I am of the opinion that the average reader is more concerned with the desire to be imaginably transported as nearly as possible to the heart of the struggle,—to live in his own mind the strain and turmoil of the individual soldier in the desperate conflict which now rages, the decision of which will determine whether democracy or military autocracy shall be the predominating factor in the governments of the peoples of the earth.

INTRODUCTORY

The devastating rush of the gray-clad hordes of Huns into the peace-loving lands of Belgium and France has demonstrated conclusively that to win this or any other war the one thing necessary is superiority in artillery. Without this, an enemy sufficiently strong in numbers and other equipment, can drive ahead, overcoming and crushing all obstacles.

The average lay reader is too apt to lose sight of the supreme importance of this arm of the service, to which all other movements are subsidiary; the dash of the charge by the infantry over the top, magnificent in its appeal, submerges to a degree the real factor upon which success or failure of the charge depends, i.e., the blazing of the trail by the guns. Little thought is devoted to the man who, with hell bursting on and around him, has to get his shell home in a certain number of seconds so that the charge can be made.

Neither is it generally known that the percentage of loss in units is greater in the unit known as the sacrifice battery than in any other branch of the fighting machine.

Therefore, I may be pardoned if I feel a certain human pride in the fact that it was my honorable lot to serve in this unit nearly a score of times during my work over there, and I can account for my failure to be seriously injured (a dislocation or a little gassing is comparatively trivial) to nothing other than, as my Major emphatically expressed it, "Damned horseshoe luck!"

CONTENTS

I. CAN'T KILL ME
II. THE FIRST NIGHT
III. YPRES
IV. MY HORSE SHOE WORKING
V. HUN HELPERS
VI. BITS OF BATTLE
VII. SANCTUARY WOODS
VIII. A BATH UNDER DIFFICULTIES
IX. HAM BONE DAVIS
X. BEES, HONEY AND HELL
XI. SCOTTY COMES BACK AT THE SOMME
XII. BEHEMOTH
XIII. THE FAMILY LUCK
XIV. THE DEAD SHELL
XV. SATAN'S SHELLS AND SCENTED GAS
XVI. BEFORE VIMY
XVII. VIMY
XVIII. BACK TO GOD'S COUNTRY

S.O.S. Stand to!

CHAPTER I
CAN'T KILL ME

"Hello, Central, give me Queen 4000. Is that you, Burt? You are going, aren't you?"

Burt Young was one of my pals and I had just learned from the morning paper that enlistments for Canada's first overseas contingent were being taken that day and I had called up to inquire if he were going.

"Sure, I am going. Where will I meet you?"

We arranged to meet at the exhibition ground and, taking French leave of the office, I hastened to the camp where the recruiting was going on, picking up Burt on the way.

It was as if a baseball championship series were on; the crowd good-naturedly swayed and jammed as each man struggled to get to the door and signed up before the quota was full. With only the loss of a hat and some slight disarrangement of my collar and tie, I was one of the lucky ones.

And we were lucky! Although visions of lands to be seen and adventures to be had flitted rapidly through my mind, and although I believe none of us on that day dreamed of what we were getting into, yet, looking back over it all, I would not have missed my place in Canada's First Division for anything I ever hope to have on earth.

In two hours I was in khaki and in another hour I had bade the folks farewell and was standing on the station platform waiting for the train that would take us to Valcartier, the greatest gathering place of soldiers that Canada has ever known.

Some idea of my knowledge of things military may be gleaned from the following:—chatting with Burt, he suddenly espied a large car, with two girls, shooting up the street to the station, and called my attention to it. One of the girls was my sister. I immediately scented trouble. I skipped across to the other side of the depot, intending to board the train from the other side when it came in; I was not going to have my soldiering interfered with if I could help it. Standing in the shelter of a pillar, I did not notice two husky recruits in khaki behind me. "Is your name Grant?" they asked. "Yes." "The Colonel wants to see you at once," they informed me, and they marched me back.

As I approached, my sister was talking earnestly and energetically to the Colonel and I could plainly see I was the object of the conversation. I waited.

"How is this, Grant, this lady says you are not of age. Is that so?" asked the Colonel.

"I am of age and—"

"Stand to attention!" snapped the Colonel. I straightened up and folded my arms respectfully across my chest.

"Stand to attention, damn you! Don't you know how to stand to attention?" I shifted my feet a little uneasily, wondering how he wanted me to stand.

"Put those heels together," he snorted. I did so. "Keep your toes apart," he half hissed and half shouted. I spread my toes apart. I still had my arms folded. Almost purple in the face with his violence, he roared, "Put those damned hands of yours down!" and he grabbed my wrists and flopped them down. "Young lady, you'll have to take this matter up at Valcartier; there is no time to do anything now. You can go," this to me. I turned on my heel.

"Here," he roared. "Don't you know enough to salute your superior officer? Salute!" I gingerly raised my hand to my forehead and held it there, much after the fashion, I think, of a man shading his eyes from the sun, or a nautical chap gazing intently seaward.

"You idiot!" he bellowed, as he grabbed my hand and fiercely flung it down. "Don't you know how to salute? Here, do this"—and he saluted. I followed as well as I was able, but the utter disgust that was plastered all over his visage as he turned on his heel would not have left much hope for soldierly qualifications in one any less hopeful and enthusiastic than I was.

S.O.S. Stand to!

My sister, in spite of her tears, could not keep back the smile as I again kissed her good-by.

It was about noon next day when I reached Valcartier and after a month of solid work, the like of which I had never before experienced, I was as hard as a nail, and as tough, as indeed was every man in that honor division of Canada's expeditionary forces.

We received orders to leave for England on the 14th day of September, 1914. I was detailed on a gun limber of my subsection of the First Battery, the artillery being the arm of the service to which I was assigned. Starting about 4:30 in the afternoon, in torrents of rain, we headed for the city of Quebec. Along the way the people had thoughtfully built large bonfires on either side of the road, serving the double purpose of lighting our way during the night and enabling us to jump off and warm ourselves, as we were thoroughly chilled.

The road was in a horribly bad condition and the rain did not improve it any, and while the limber was lurching from side to side, like a ship staggering in a storm, it was the better part of wisdom for me to keep my eyes open to save myself from being thrown off and having my precious neck broken.

To prevent in some measure the rain trickling down my neck, I took a rubber sheet, used to cover the horses, tied the two corners together, making a sort of cape of it, and put it round my neck.

Then I settled myself down to hold on to the limber and think at the same time of the great game of which I had become an infinitesimal part. I was sitting on the right hand side of the limber close to the wheel and, before long, the effort to think and hold on at the same time was too much for me, and I fell into a fairly sound sleep, Sergeant Johnson, my companion, doing likewise.

While dozing, the string from the end of the cape engaged itself with the axle, wound itself round and round and started pulling me down. When I awoke it had a grip on me and every moment I was being drawn closer to the wheel. I yelled to the driver to stop the horse, but the rattling and rumble of the limber and the gun carriage

S.O.S. Stand to!

drowned my call; neither he nor the Sergeant heard me. Numb with cold, absolutely helpless, my head almost down to the wheel, I gave one more yell for dear life. The Sergeant suddenly and providentially woke up; he thought he had a nightmare. I was almost choked and could hardly breathe, but managed to make him understand, and he whipped out his knife, cut the string and released me from what in a couple of seconds more would have been instant death, as I would have been pulled from my seat and crushed to a jelly between the wheels. This was my first close shave from death. I had no horseshoe or four-leaf clover with me, and I can account for my escape in no other way than that it was my lucky star that has accompanied me throughout the long months of times that try men's souls and that has never deserted me.

No further mishaps befell until I was safely aboard ship. I was in charge of a fatigue party, bringing hay from the bulkheads of the ship up on to the different decks for the horses; there was a pulley leading to the bottom of the boat by means of which the hay was hoisted up, and in going down each man gripped it and was slowly lowered. On the trip down the men would cling to the rope, two or three at a time, with about ten to twenty feet of space between them. In making a downward trip I was second; the man ahead of me going down was over twenty feet from me; and the rope suddenly slipping off the pulley and out of the hands of the men running it, I dropped fifty feet. The man below on the rope broke his leg and on top of him I fell. Although my drop was twenty or thirty feet longer than his, on account of the space between us being that much greater, I was none the worse except for a bad shaking-up. Like all the men in Canada's First Division, my pal was in excellent physical shape, and it was not long before his leg mended and he was himself again. Nothing of further moment happened until we heard the welcome call of land!

The different batteries were ordered to remove their guns, limbers and horses from the boat, and I had charge of one party unloading guns and limbers. A derrick and cable was used to lift our pets from the vessel's hold, swing them up across the side of the boat and over on to the dock. In my duty I was stationed on the dock, catching hold of the guns and wagons as they were swung out and over by the

S.O.S. Stand to!

derrick, and pulling them across on to the dock. While pulling over a gun, the cable skidded and the gun, coming on top of me, caught me partly under it, knocking me unconscious. Luckily the weight of the gun did not fall on me in its entirety; if it had, I would not be telling this story; it caught me on the hip, dislocating the hip bone. I was removed to the ship's hospital and was under the doctor's care till morning, and from there I went to a hospital in Plymouth City for six weeks. From there I was removed to the field general hospital in Salisbury Plain, where I tarried an additional ten days. While here I had a two-fold adventure.

The hospital was in a tent where I reclined with forty other patients, and directly opposite our tent was another in which were confined under guard a number of patients who were subject to fits, some of a very serious nature. Lying in bed, my leg encased in its plaster-of-paris cast, about ten o'clock one night, when just dozing off, I was frightened into wakefulness by a scream. A man, who turned out to be an escaped epileptic, was standing in the doorway screaming, his eyes bulging out of his head. He had escaped by striking the sentry over the head with the fire brazier, used to keep the sentry warm. Staring wildly about the room for a couple of seconds, he made a leap for the nearest man and bit him in the arm; he then jumped at the next patient, biting him; I was the following recipient of his devotions, getting a bite on the wrist. Utterly unable to help or defend myself, as I was bound down in my plaster-of-paris cast, I had to content myself with landing a couple of punches on his mad mug, but he didn't seem to mind them in the least,—rather enjoyed them, I fancy.

By way of diversion he then took hold of the beds and started upsetting them, rolling the patients out on to the floor, causing a tremendous amount of excitement, as well as pain and suffering to the men upset who, some of them, like myself, had casts on their limbs. In the midst of his mad capers the guard and orderlies rushed in, but before he was subdued he managed to fasten his molars in the arm of a guard.

A bite from a man in his condition is no laughing matter and the doctors took no chances; every man who was bitten had the wound immediately and thoroughly cauterized and was inoculated.

S.O.S. Stand to!

My other adventure was the honor and pleasure of receiving a handshake from their Majesties, the King and Queen of England, who were on a visit of inspection to the camp. The visit of their Majesties was concluded by a splendid little speech from Queen Alexandra in which she complimented us and thanked us for our loyalty.

After my release from the hospital due to the effects of the accident at Plymouth, I set to work looking after our horses and performing general battery work. After my narrow escape from the gun wheel, the fall into the hold of the vessel and the close shave I had had on the dock, I was commencing to wonder whether I was destined ever to get to France.

Thus musing, I was riding one of the horses bare-back to a small creek to give it a watering, and the rein, which was a long one, I held in my right hand. I had to pass the targets where shooting practice was going on, and the brute, taking fright, gave a sudden leap and threw me off his back. I fell backwards and on the left side, and as I fell the long rein wound itself round my right arm, keeping me tied as it were to the horse; and my head came dangerously close to the animal's front hoofs which he was kicking up every other second; with each jump he took, those hoofs, in their upward motion of making a spring, almost struck my face. I was dragged helpless for about twenty feet when, providentially, the rein broke and I dropped to the ground, the horse dashing on in his fright until he was finally captured.

I was picked up for dead and a stretcher was sent for; but, while on the way, consciousness returned and in a few minutes I was able to navigate without assistance. I then and there decided that I surely was preserved for France and was not doomed to die an ignominious or untimely death behind the front line trenches.

After supper that night I listened to the remarkable story of a man whose lot was destined to be woven with mine to a degree:—"Aye, laddie, they came on thick at Mons! There was one time there when there was only Sandy MacFarlane and mysel' left out o' the whole company, and for two or three hours we lay behind a wee bank, no higher'n your knee, fighting them off. Lord how we plugged them!

S.O.S. Stand to!

They died like flies! And then puir Sandy got his, an' there was naething left for me tae do but tae beat an honorable retreat, an' I grabbed Sandy's rifle an' retired on to the main body, wi' the bullets buzzin' like bees around me. On my way back I loaded both rifles as quick as I could and dropped every noo an' again to let them hae it, and I was carefu' not to waste a damn shot; every bullet told."

The speaker was Scotty Henderson, late of the Seaforth Highlanders, as he informed us, and he was relating his experiences during the world memorable retreat at Mons, when Britain's little regular army, denominated by His Majesty, Wilhelm II, "The contemptible little English army," was practically wiped out.

In the cookhouse we listened, open-mouthed, to the wonderful exploits of this Scotch fighting man. "Were you wounded?" asked Lawrence. "Aye, laddie, you're damned right I was," and he rolled up his trouser leg and exhibited a large, broad scar on the inside of his right leg. "There's where I got it."

"That's a funny looking wound,—looks like a burn," said Lawrence.

"You're damned right it's a burn," said Scotty, "it was the shell that burned me as it grazed my leg."

The probable reason, I thought, why the shell could graze the inside of one of his legs without injury to the other was because the fighter was blessed with a pair of bow-legs that couldn't have stopped the proverbial pig in the proverbial alley. In addition to this decided detraction from his manly beauty, he was short, squatty, thick-necked, a nose of the variety commonly known as a stub, and a couple of little eyes that had a constant twinkle, half-shrewd and half-humorous, the whole surmounted with a shock of shaggy red hair. But these detractions from his beauty did not in the least lessen our admiration for his personal bravery; he was in our eyes a first-class fighting man; he had proven it by his work at Mons and had the scar to show for it.

"But how did you come to get into a Canadian unit?" asked another.

"Well, you see, after I was wounded in the leg and got my honorable discharge, as soon as I was well, I wanted to do my bit again, and knowing that you laddies get bigger pay than in the British army, I thought I would kill two birds wi' the one stone,—get more money and get into the game again. So I ups and goes to the Colonel and says I, 'Colonel, I'd like to get into the game again.' 'Well,' says he, 'I hae na room for any more men in my command, but I do want a gude cook,' an' it just happened that I was a cook by trade, and a gude one too, and told him so, and says he, 'Well, you're just the man I want,' and he signed me up there and then, and here I am."

He was a good cook and he was proud of it too; we had no reason to complain of the way our meals were prepared. There was only one thing about Scotty that caused a shade of dissatisfaction,—he was so scrupulously careful to see that no man got more than his just share of the grub that many a fellow grumbled about not getting enough to eat and, in many cases, that they did not get what was coming to them. But Scotty would shut them with the authority of an old soldier and, besides, in his cookhouse he was monarch of all he surveyed. In a half-humorous, half-scolding voice he would say, "Mon, what do you want to be a hog for? Do you want to let someone else gang hungry? Tak' what's given ye and thank God you're alive to eat it, because it won't be long maybe before you'll be where ye won't need any grub—although undoubtedly you'll need water."

This was an allusion to our probable future abode. So we had to be content with what he chose to serve us. But there were speculations by some as to whether or not Scotty really served us all the grub given him by the quartermaster's department, and someone was so unjust, I thought, as to venture the suggestion that he believed "the damned Scotch runt is selling the grub to men in other units." "How does it happen," said he, in support of his suspicion, "that he always has a little change when the rest of us are broke?"

"Oh, nonsense," said I, "a good soldier wouldn't do such a thing, and we all know he is a good soldier; there is no getting away from that."

CHAPTER II
THE FIRST NIGHT

I arrived in France early in February, 1915, and for three weeks we were put into the hands of an Imperial battery, the Warwicks. They had taken part in the battle of Mons, and the tales of the veterans of this world's memorable retreat, told in their own modest way, gave me my first clear impression as to what the boys of the Imperial Army really had endured for civilization in that campaign.

At first I thought they were trying to bluff us Colonials, but the first night I was in the lines I realized in the largest degree of human intensity the fearful truth of their experiences.

The tuition given us by these warriors could not be excelled. They took us to Fleurbaix, where their batteries were located on the outskirts of the town, in cellars in the back part of a building destroyed by German fire. There they had skillfully transformed the cellar into a gun pit, with a loophole four feet in diameter overlooking an orchard at the rear. Each time the gun spoke it would first be shoved into the hole and the brush and sandbags removed, and as quickly as the message was sent, the camouflage was replaced.

The color of the sandbags was a rusty gray and this, in conjunction with the brushwood, prevented the spot taking on a dark appearance, which, next to white, is the most easily distinguishable to an airplane; the air birds are always on the lookout for these dark spots, watching them intently to discover if any signs of activity are there, and immediately anything smacking of life appears, the exact location is wired to their trenches and the place is whirlwinded with showers of death and destruction.

When the Warwicks had completed our educational course, there was no detail of handling the guns with which we were not acquainted, and thoroughly so, and I had the honor of being in charge of my gun, due to the accuracy in my work. I think my chest expansion increased a trifle, but my cap did not get any smaller.

S.O.S. Stand to!

At the end of ten days we left Meteren, arriving there February 28. It was on the way from Meteren that I received my battle christening; the ceremony was performed by a bevy of six airplanes, two of them flying low and doing the sprinkling honors with a fusillade of bombs, dropped on the road round about us. They left twenty or twenty-five of these calling cards, but two of the batteries of anti-aircraft guns handled by the Warwicks greeted them so warmly that they quickly decided they had overstaid their welcome and made a hurried departure.

When the battery arrived at its designated point, we proceeded to camouflage the guns with the artistry we had derived from our instruction, covering them securely with grass and brushwood.

It was at this time that I lost not only my increased chest expansion, but also a trifle more, because I was ordered to take my gun to a position known as the sacrifice gun position, three hundred yards back of the front line trench. It derives its name, "sacrifice gun," from the fact that rarely, if ever, in case of a heavy enemy raid, does the gun or any of its crew escape. This "honor" I was destined to receive many times throughout my career in the Great Adventure.

I was in charge of the gun and I installed it in a hedge. The only time we were to fire was when the enemy broke through and when our men in retreating were on a line even with us; and we could not fire until we got orders from the officer commanding or from headquarters.

The idea of a sacrifice gun is this: if the enemy broke through on either or both flanks, pushing our men back, we had to wait for orders from the commanding officer or from headquarters before firing; All the ammunition carried was fifty shells; it was all we could get in those days. In daytime the gun was covered with brush and other means of concealment to keep it from the ever watchful eye of the Hun. At night the crew consisted of two men, one on each side of the gun, and three more in a ruined building a hundred yards in the rear of the gun. Our shifts were two hours on and four off. The purpose pursued by the sacrifice gun is to surprise the enemy when in full view and exposed, killing as many of them as possible, blasting gaps through their line and enabling our men to dig in in

S.O.S. Stand to!

the position to which they have retired, we knowing all the while that there is not one chance in a thousand that the men connected with the sacrifice gun will escape either death or capture. Our orders were under no circumstances to leave the gun as long as a shell remained and a man lived. Deuced pleasant! The ground in front of us was well drilled with concealed holes all the way from four to six feet deep, in each of which strands of barbed wire had been placed and the opening carefully concealed with clumps of grass, brush and the like.

Blaisdell and I volunteered to take first shift on the gun on the first night, about 10 o'clock. We had to take a narrow path on the way, with Fritz sniping us every step; he had registered the path and it was a constant target for his machine guns and snipers. Our pet was well hidden in the hedge, with its nose poking through a hole in the leafage and so cunningly camouflaged that it was absolutely impossible to be noticed.

While lying stretched on each side of the gun between the muzzle and wheel, any talking we did was to whisper cautiously to each other, as the very grass beneath our feet contained spies in those days; the country-side round about was as thickly infested with them as cells in a honeycomb; and thus we waited.

Presently we heard the crackle of a piece of brushwood immediately out in our front. The intruder had gotten into our entanglement. "Halt! Who goes there?" No answer. I repeated the challenge; still no answer. We made our way cautiously through the hedge, unclicked our safety catches and were just about to fire in the direction of the sound when someone yelled, "Where's the Durham Light Infantry lying?" We ordered them to advance until within ten feet.

"Who are you?"

"Durham Light Infantry."

In the darkness we could not tell who they were but they spoke English like natives.

"What are you doing out here wandering around in this fashion?"

"Well," one of them answered, "we were taking a stroll and got lost and we want to find our way back."

We directed them and when they were lost sight of in the darkness, we resumed our places on each side of the gun and thought no more of the incident for the time. We again installed ourselves comfortably and were comparatively safe from the sniping in front, which was going on more or less all the time we were there, and about thirty minutes had elapsed when, in the silence of the night, I thought I again heard the crackling of a twig. Blaisdell heard it too. "Hist! Did you hear that, Grant?"

"Yes," I whispered.

We listened intently and heard it again, this time a little closer. We jumped up.

"Halt! Who goes there?"

No answer. Bang! Blaisdell fired, and these same fellows called, "Don't shoot! We're looking for the Durhams." We emerged through the hedge.

"What in hell are you fellows doing around here again?" I asked.

"Well, we can't find the Durham Light Infantry."

"Well, you find some place away from here if you want to live to eat your breakfast. If I find you around here again I'll shoot without warning."

Again they asked us the way and again we directed them, and saw them started on their way to the rear.

Once more we took our places on the gun between the wheels and were hardly settled down when a sniper opened up on us from the rear, taking a chip out of the wheel to my right. Ping! Ping! Ping! and the tree standing ten feet in our rear was nipped. Ping! Ping! and the shield of the gun got it this time. We were concealed behind the gun shield, which protected us pretty thoroughly from the front fire and were congratulating ourselves on our haven of safety when Ping! Ping! again from our rear came the messages from a sniper hidden

S.O.S. Stand to!

there. In glancing back over my shoulder I noticed in the pitchy blackness the flash of a rifle simultaneously with the report, and it seemed to come from a haystack about 200 yards to our right.

"Blais, look back for a minute and tell me what you see."

Black darkness again for a few minutes, then another flare; we both watched intently.

"By God!" exclaimed Blaisdell simultaneously with another report. "Right out of the stack!" There was nothing for us to do but to lie there and watch, and we absolutely confirmed our convictions that we were being sniped at from this particular haystack.

When our watch was up I made my way to the ruin occupied by our relief, woke them and told them to keep their eyes open for the haystack and make themselves as small as midgets. Shortly after they started, Blaisdell came in. He told me that the relief party had been sniped at every step of the way to the gun. As Blaisdell entered, the open door threw out a fitful glare of light from our flickering candle, and a report from this particular haystack was followed by a bullet that knocked off a chip of brick just above the doorway. Our friend was certainly industrious, but I hoped to go him one better in the morning. I grabbed the phone and called up headquarters, informing them of what I had seen from the stock. The O.C. said the matter would be looked into immediately.

There was no sleeping that night; we were too excited and chattered away like school girls over our experiences, and to pass the time the inevitable card game started. During the game the sniping was active and continuous, the bullets chipping the building in all quarters. Our light was from a candle jammed into a jam tin and set between a couple of sand bags that we used for a table. Our mate, who had not yet taken his turn on the gun-watch, was inclined to be rather skeptical about our story of the sniper, declaring it couldn't be possible that Fritzie could be carrying on such work in the very midst of our lines, and that our imaginations had been running riot with us. We had been playing about three-quarters of an hour when a gust of wind blew the door open, throwing the faint gleam of the candle out in front. I jumped to close the door, the light blowing out

S.O.S. Stand to!

as I did so, and at the same instant I heard a report from the same direction as before. I closed the door, telling Blaisdell to light the candle. He fumbled for his matches and lit it, and we were both stricken dumb for the moment; our chum was lying stone dead with a hole squarely in his forehead. The gentleman in the haystack was surely doing good work for his Kaiser.

Just before daylight we had a call from the O.C., accompanied by three or four men; he had phoned us he was coming. He wanted all particulars regarding my previous message. Under cover of the hedge we got to within fifty yards of the stack and everybody was convinced of the certainty of the information I had given, for, as we watched, two more flashes came from the stack. Not a particle of doubt was left and the officer ordered a bomb thrown into the haystack. Inside of a minute the red flames began shooting out from all sides, in another minute it was ablaze, and in five minutes we had the joy and satisfaction of hearing the muffled shriek of the soldier who had so well served his Kaiser.

This ended for me a busy first night in the front line.

When the ashes of the fire were searched we found the charred body of a man, the remains of a rifle and a complete set of telephone apparatus, which was traced to our trenches, and from there to the German lines.

Wilhelm for a certainty lost an ace in the haystack. Besides our chum and heavens knows what others, he had sniped the road along which relief parties were passing up and down; and that same night one of the soldiers of an infantry battalion of the Warwicks, winding its way to the front trenches, got his death from a bullet squarely in the neck; and the Germans having through him gotten an absolutely accurate range, our gun was wiped out by a single shell, together with two members of the crew.

Next afternoon, while resting in billets to where I had been ordered, a shell struck the building, a splinter knocking out the eye of Ed. Jackson, who was sitting beside me. He was not killed, but his wound was a blighty, taking him out of the game for good. The unwelcome visitors continuing to come, we were rushed to our

S.O.S. Stand to!

battery of three guns in an orchard near by; a curtain of sandbags was placed in front to prevent the flash being seen. As soon as we started firing, rifle shots from our left scattered the mud on all sides, coming at intervals of five or ten minutes. Speculation was aroused and we set a man to watch, and suspicion fastened on a farmer who was working his plow. Nothing was found on him. Next day the same thing happened and again the watch was set. This time our efforts were rewarded; the scout saw the farmer shoot and throw the rifle down. He reported to the officer and we went over. The horny-handed son of toil was very busy at the plow as he saw us coming. He couldn't speak English. The officer sent to the nearest French battery and presently a French soldier came who interpreted the officer's questions and the man's replies. He knew nothing, whatever, he said, about the rifle shots coming from his direction.

A search was then made for the rifle where the scout had seen him throw it and not only one rifle, but several, including English, French and German makes, were found in various parts of the field, partly buried in the soil. When the guns were discovered the farmer threw up his hands, wildly gesticulating and vehemently protesting that he knew nothing whatever as to how they came there. His was a short shrift. He was tried on the spot, tied to the pump of his own farm and shot.

CHAPTER III
YPRES

I remained in this spot with the guns until March, when the costly victory of Neuve Chapelle was fought. My battery was playing on their northern flank. The objective of the British Tommies was the city, which they took, but at a terrible toll; 6,000 Indian troops, mostly Ghurkas, were slain. The fearful mortality exacted from these troops was due to their impetuosity; they do not know fear; it was impossible to hold them; they rushed out before their time and some of them suffered from the fire of our own guns. It was in this fight that our own famous and gallant regiment, the "Princess Pats," was decimated, sustaining a loss of over 700 men. This magnificent body of fellows went into the war 1,150 strong and at the last roll call but 22 of the original men answered. The price paid was too much for what was accomplished.

We were then ordered to billets and stayed there until April 20th, when we were ordered to Ypres, arriving there April 21. My battery was stationed at St. Julien, one and a half miles northwest of the city. Here I was detailed as observer, my duty being to get into the front-line trench and from the most advantageous nook that I could find, try to discover whatever I could about the movement of the enemy, communicate my knowledge to the telephonist who would in turn send it to headquarters.

Late in the afternoon I reported to the telephonist that a big fire was in progress somewhere on our left, as an immense smoke cloud was rising there and coming toward us. As shells had burst his wire, rendering it useless, he started out to deliver the message by word of mouth, running on top of the parapet as he started. That was the last I ever saw of him; he did not come back; Fritz was coming and ahead of him rolled the sinister-looking cloud on our left. Then happened the strangest thing! The line trembled from one end to the other, as the Algerian troops immediately on our left, jumped out of their trenches, falling as they ran. The whole thing seemed absolutely incomprehensible—until I got a whiff of the gas. They ran like men possessed, gasping, choking, blinded and dropping with suffocation.

S.O.S. Stand to!

They could hardly be blamed. It was a new device in warfare and thoroughly illustrative of the Prussian idea of playing the game.

When the great yellow clouds came rolling toward us, orders were roared to wet our handkerchiefs and stuff them in our mouths, and half choked and blinded we held for a day and a half. The buttons on our uniforms were tinged yellow and green from the gas, so virulent was the poison.

Cooks and everybody else had been ordered into the line, as the giving way of the Algerians necessitated our lengthening out so as to take over their ground. Scotty of Mons fame was in the trench bay a few yards away from me, and when the cloud had passed by I saw him rolling on the ground, apparently blinded, tears streaming from his eyes. I helped him to his feet and when he got his voice back his courage returned and, yelling, "Let the barbarians come," he seized his rifle, rushed to the parapet and fired point blank every cartridge in his rifle in the direction of Fritz.

At the end of the second day another wave of hell's atmosphere came across, more deadly than any of the others, followed by a smothering fire from the German batteries, and the Germans broke in upon us on our right and left. Yard by yard we retreated, fighting as we went, and they occupied some of our front trenches—for a time.

A Chlorine Gas Attack from the Trenches

S.O.S. Stand to!

That night Scotty and I received orders to report to a French dressing station for treatment. I half-dragged and half-walked him to the doctor; I had a feeling that he ought to have been able to make the trip without my help as I was certain he wasn't suffering any more than I was. After we left the doctor and got outside the dressing station, Scotty swayed from side to side, groaning like a man who had lost his last hope on earth, and the doctor told him to get away as quickly as he could as he was playing the devil with the nerves of the men who were lying around there half-dead from the poison fumes. He staggered over and sat down beside me on the side of the road, still wringing his hands. I remonstrated with him and told him that bad as it was it could not be anything like Mons, and to my amazement he stopped his moaning all at once and said with a twinkle in his eye, "Let's beat it to the dugout; the doc won't see us." We took the chance and started. On the way Fritz shot up the road and with a spring like an india-rubber man, Scotty jumped behind a tree. We finally reached our destination and Scotty proceeded to get something to eat. He lit a fire while I brought the water. The cookhouse here was in the house of a farmer who had vacated, and as the smoke coming from the chimney got thicker every moment, I was apprehensive lest Fritz would see it and send over a shell message, but Scotty pooh-poohed the idea.

Dinner was almost ready when—Kr-kr-kr-p! Kr-kr-kr-p! Bang! and a shell shot clean through the joint. The concussion threw me to the floor, covering me with lime and plaster-of-paris from the walls and ceiling. I got up and looked around for the cook. The hero of Mons had been knocked down, with the stove on top of him, and he was lying in the corner praying like a good fellow. "Oh, Lord! look down in pity and save me! Thou knowest, Lord, I am unworthy o' thy mercy, but please control the shells o' those barbarians and send them in anither direction, and Thine shall be a' the glory." Then he saw me standing there and he yelled, "Do you think there'll be any more?" "No, that was merely a stray shell. Let's get this grub, I'm starving." "Stray shell be damned," said he, "they've seen the smoke and they'll be putting more over."

No sooner said than Kr-kr-kr-p! Kr-kr-kr-p! Kr-kr-kr-p! and three or four more shells banged about the place, one of them blowing the

S.O.S. Stand to!

pump from outside through the shack past Scotty, out through the other wall, and Scotty, ducking and dodging like a man trying to buck the line in a football game, shot through the door and vanished in the night.

The pan of bacon he had been cooking was still intact except that it had a coating of plaster-of-paris from the walls and ceiling of the room, and I proceeded to put it under my belt as fast as my jaws would work, and then made for my dugout. I was just settling down to a quiet smoke when I heard the Major calling for Scotty at the top of his voice. Getting no response, he called for me and I hastened to his quarters.

"Grant, go down and see if that Scotch cook has fallen in the soup; find out if cookhouse is ready." "Yes, sir." I said nothing about what had happened and returned to the cookhouse to find six Algerians devouring the officers' rations in such fashion as to make one think of the man in the side show who was advertised in letters twenty feet deep as the original snake-eater of South America; there wasn't enough left for a one-man meal. I reported to the O.C. that there were no signs of Scotty but that the cookhouse had been hit by a shell.

"Go and see if he is at the dressing station." I went back to the station. For nearly a mile the wounded and gassed men were lying on each side of the road waiting for conveyances to remove them. I spoke to a Tommy who had met with a peculiar accident; he had two plates in his mouth and the concussion of a shell explosion in his immediate vicinity had broken the plates into four pieces, leaving him practically toothless.

Strongly suspecting by that time that if Scotty were anywhere on earth he was at the rear in the wagon line, I waited around the station just long enough to lend plausibility to my search before reporting to the O.C. The Major was in a towering rage over our losses, and, damning the cook, he dismissed me. The officers that night had to look to another cookhouse for their evening meal.

Next morning I was sent for by the Major and dispatched to the wagon lines on an errand;—at that time I was fulfilling the duties of a runner for our unit;—he also told me to have a lookout for the cook while there and make some inquiries about him. I saluted and left. The first place I went to in the wagon lines was the cookhouse and as I got there I thought I noticed the swish of someone quickly disappearing round the corner and the cockney-cook there informed me that Scotty had spent the previous evening with them and had only left a minute ago.

"'E's no slouch, that cook of yours," he said, "'e's a fighter, 'e is."

"That so?"

"You're right, 'e is. Wy, where 'e was stationed, when the Germans rushed 'em in the trench, 'e 'eld 'em back, killin' two of 'em single-handed until the others had retreated. 'E ought to get the D.C.M., 'e ought; that's what hi say. By Gawd! when it comes to the real thing, give me the Scotch! An' honly last night 'e was in his cookhouse with some blighter by the name of Grant when the shells came along, and this fellow must have 'ad a streak of yellow for he promised to 'elp Scotty with the meal, but bolted like a bullet at the first shell."

"How did he come to be down here?" I asked.

"Wy, he got relieved."

"Where is he now?"

"Hover in the dugout."

I learned that the hero of Mons had regaled them with accounts of his feats of valor in the trenches, very similar to the tales he had recounted to us at Salisbury Plain of his achievements in the Great Retreat, and the cook had given him a meal befitting a hero of his caliber, which Scotty had devoured with the relish and avidity of four heroes, while the others had shown him the due and necessary deference becoming a man of action.

For the benefit of the cook I informed him that Scotty was a damned liar; that it was I who had been with him; that he ran like a white-livered cur under fire from his cookhouse and didn't stop until he had reached the wagon lines; that he was there without being relieved and that he would shortly have another tale to tell.

I hastened to the dugout he had indicated as Scotty's retreat and found him in the innermost corner, pretending to be asleep; he didn't answer until I called him three or four times.

"Scotty, the O.C. wants to know why you left the cookhouse without guard permitting some Algerians to eat up his bacon and stuff, and, further, why you ran away under fire. You are in for hell as sure as there is heather in your hair." His countenance took on a greenish hue and he mumbled something about being shell-shocked and refused to come. I persuaded him, however, to come over to the Quartermaster of the wagon line, and that officer asked him what he was doing there.

"Weel,—I was wounded and couldna' fight anither stroke; I was jeest tired oot wi' killin' Boches and hadna' the strength to stand anither minute; I jeest had to get away."

"Well, you've had a damned good rest now and you can get back to the O.C. and tell him what you have told me and he will see that you get a fitting decoration." This latter was spoken very grimly, and I could see the great fighter's face fall. "You will see to it, Grant," said the Q.M. "that Henderson doesn't hide his heroism from the O.C.; that he gives it to him in detail, just as he has to me." "Yes, sir," and I left with my prisoner.

We hurried along as night was falling and the German flares were commencing to fly. On the way back we met two Algerian troopers and in the gleam of a star shell and the fading twilight they looked more like two escaped denizens of the chamber of horrors than anything I could well imagine. Indeed, their appearance was so ghastly under the weird light of the flares and the fading day, that I involuntarily shivered, hardened though I was by that time to grim sights. Each of them carried on his shoulder the hind-quarter of a cow that had been killed by a shell at a nearby farm, and the dripping blood from the beast had slopped all over their uniforms; under each arm was tucked a ham they had "swiped" from the farmhouse and each had a young suckling pig running ahead, squealing and grunting, tied by a string on the hind leg and held by the left hand, while in the right hand each man carried a sharply pointed stick to prod the pig when it veered from a straight line, which was about every other step or so.

Just as we got immediately opposite the looters a burst of shell fire from the German guns, followed by a hail of shrapnel, blazed all about us, and the hero-cook jumped like a bullfrog, bumping plumb into one of the Algerians, and he and the cook and the pig tumbled over and over, the pig squealing like mad, the Algerian rolling out deep-throated oaths in his native tongue, and Scotty cursing as only a redheaded gabby Scotchman can, all amid an ear-splitting din of shrieking shells and flare-gleams completing a *mise en scène* as striking as anything ever created by a master artist of stagecraft.

When Scotty extricated himself from the tangle his face and clothes were smeared from the blood of the dripping beast, so that he could indeed have passed for the blood-stained hero he had proclaimed himself in the cookhouse, and in spite of his plight Scotty grinned as I suggested the thought to him and the twinkle returned to his eye, and his spirits took a decidedly upward turn until we reached the Major's quarters.

The Major was still cursing mad over the loss of the trenches in the gas attack and I felt the moment he spoke that Scotty's fate looked black.

"Where have you been, Henderson?"

"I was in the cookhouse, sir, when a shell struck it, smashing everything in sight, and I lost complete control o' my nerves and started for the wagon lines wi'out knowing what I was doing or where I was going, and didna' come to mysel' until Grant ran across me in the dugout."

"That won't go, Henderson. Orderly room at ten-thirty in the morning. It's the first case of cowardice in this unit and I'll take damned good care that it will be the last. Grant, escort the prisoner back to the wagon lines."

S.O.S. Stand to!

I could not help feeling sorry for the poor devil because, coward though he was, his was one of those personalities that carried with it a sort of likeableness, somewhat after the fashion of our time-honored Falstaff, and his funk under fire made him liable to the extreme penalty,—a firing squad. His teeth chattered like the keys of a typewriter as he asked me, "What do you think will come o' it, Grant? Do you think he really means it?"

I hadn't the heart to tell him what I really thought and strove to jolly him by saying that the Major would feel in a better humor in the morning, "and besides," said I, "when we take back those trenches tomorrow, he will get over his flurry."

I turned my prisoner over to the guard of the wagon lines, first informing the Quartermaster, and when he asked me what the trouble was, I had to tell him of the variance of the prisoner's story told him and that he told the Major, and that the Major directed that he be up for orderly room in the morning. Without any further ceremony Scotty was jammed in the clink.

It was now almost daybreak of the morning of the third day following our first gas attack and, almost ready to drop with fatigue, I went over to the wagon lines, gathered some straw and bags together under an ammunition wagon, and was in a dead sleep in less time than it takes to tell it.

At ten-thirty I reported to the orderly room to attend Scotty's trial. The Major was in his appointed place and in due course the guard marched in with the prisoner. His ammunition pouches and cap had been removed and he stood to attention as well as the contour of his legs and the thickness of his yellow streak permitted. Still I could not help remembering what he had done at Mons; there was no doubt about that because I had seen his scar and I knew that the ranks of the Seaforth Highlanders had never held a coward; and I mentally concluded that he must really have been suffering from shell shock or he would never have left his post as he did, and I sincerely hoped that he would in some way get through. The evidence was short and conclusive and the verdict was curt and decisive:—"held in close confinement for general field court martial at Steenwercke, May 12."

S.O.S. Stand to!

And Scotty was led out looking as if he hadn't a friend in the world; there was very little sympathy for him from anyone.

The same evidence was repeated at the field court martial trial, but the twinkle in Scotty's eye must have reached the heart of the commanding officer for he was ordered deported to England, pending dishonorable discharge. There he was sent to the military camp at Shorncliffe, put under open arrest and utilized around the camp in a number of ways for over a year.

That afternoon Colonel Morrison sent for me. "Grant, run to Colonel Curry and find out how strong the Forty-eighth Highlanders and the Third Brigade are, and how soon he can get the men together for attack." "Yes, sir," and I started. I was running along the top of the canal bank in broad daylight and in the open, expecting every second that one of the missiles from the shower that was pattering the ground everywhere would get me. In that race through that bullet-swept zone I felt a common bond of kinship with the Irish soldier who was running as fast as his legs could carry him from the Battle of the Wilderness in the American Civil War and General Sherman, noticing him, turned his horse in the direction of the fleeing soldier and halted him up.

"Here, you soldier, what are you running away for?"

"Because, Gineral—because I can't fly."

How I longed for wings! The Colonel later recommended me for a commission and many times since have I wondered how he would feel about that recommendation if he ever learned the real state of my feelings at that moment. He did me the honor of requesting Colonel Morrison to permit me to enter his unit and Colonel Morrison did me the additional honor of refusing to let me go. I had gotten a somewhat painful scalp wound on the way over, and I made my way to the French dressing station in a half-unconscious condition. The French doctor nearly completed matters by spilling the iodine in my eye and nearly blinding me. Some dope was then administered that brought me to my full senses shortly after.

S.O.S. Stand to!

When I was getting fixed up at the dressing station—I had a hard time as the wounded men were swarming everywhere—I saw two women in the station carrying baskets and speaking to the soldiers. They seemed to be peasant women, but spoke very good English. They left after some little time and wended their way up the road; but something in their appearance directed attention to them and they were watched! After they had gone a little bit up the road one of them was seen to open her basket and let a pigeon go. They were at once arrested, handed over to the French police and taken to Ypres.

The work of the gendarmerie was unexcelled; they were everywhere they were needed; had it not been for their lightning-like acumen and prompt service, the Lord only knows what would have become of us poor Britishers in that country, as we were practically at the mercy of the spies, not knowing who was who.

The two women were taken to Ypres and were treated to their deserved fate—shot. But the pigeon did its work. Within an hour after their arrest the hospital was shelled; it was packed with patients and in one of the wards one of those flying ministers of death exploded, leaving not a single living man.

CHAPTER IV
MY HORSESHOE WORKING

It was the fourth day of the second battle of Ypres. I was in charge of my subsection at the guns and the men wanted water. I volunteered and went to a farmhouse 150 yards off, got the water and had started back for the guns. I had just stepped outside the door of the farmhouse when Kr-kr-kr-p! a huge shell came over and blew the gun and gun crew into kingdom come. A French captain was standing twenty feet from the door and, following the report, I started for our gun. I had just taken a step or two when another monster of death came hurtling through the air, straight for me, as I thought, but, instead, it was a message for the French soldier; it got him squarely, leaving not a fragment of his body to be seen.

Immediately after the death of our gun crew and the French captain our gun position was moved, and that same evening after supper, consisting of the usual bread, jam and tea, Walter Hope and I were on our way to the dugout. When half-way there a sudden emptiness entered into my life and the next thing I knew I was being lifted on to a stretcher. I rebelled and got to my feet. What had happened was this, as told me by one of the boys who was standing a short distance off,—a shell had come and exploded almost at my feet, throwing me in the air for a distance, as he said, of fully twenty feet. It is impossible for me to personally make an estimate of the distance, as I was unconscious when I went up and when I came down.

When I recovered my senses, Hope was hopping around holding his right hand with his left and exclaiming like a madman. His hand had been almost severed by a fragment from the shell and was hanging to the wrist by a shred. He ran to the cookhouse and the cook advised him to go at once to the dressing station, as he couldn't do anything for him; instead, in his frenzy, he ran to the gun pits, going from one to the other, looking for help. Every man there wanted to help him, but he wouldn't and couldn't stand still; the concussion of the shell had affected his brain and this accounted for his ungovernableness. Then a few of us grabbed him and I bandaged it as best I could, walked over to the road with him and started him on

S.O.S. Stand to!

his way to the dressing station; I could go no further, as we had commenced firing, and he made his way alone. When nearing the station his senses completely left him for the time and he plucked off his hanging hand and threw it from him. The poor lad was then taken into the station, properly attended to and sent to England.

Thankful am I to tell that he came through all right and is now working in Toronto earning his living by writing with his left hand, which he has learned to manipulate with practically the same agility the lost member possessed. We were deeply regretful at the loss of Hope from the crowd—fearless Hope, as he was known, and, sometimes, hopeless Hope—because never in all my experience have I seen a man who was so utterly regardless of danger; he would expose himself to what seemed certain death, and, as luck would have it, he got his blighty at a place that ordinarily would be considered about as safe from harm as could be found.

On the fifth day of the second battle of Ypres, April 25, 1915, McKay, an orderly, came up the line with ammunition for the guns as our supply was exhausted. As soon as the shells were delivered it was his duty to report at once to the Captain for further orders. The poor fellow was starving for something to eat and he thought he would steal the time to slip up to the cookhouse and get a bite of grub. He rode his horse across and was in the act of leaning over to get a couple of hardtacks the cook was handing him, when a splinter of a shell that had exploded at his horse's feet, struck him in the neck, killing him instantly, slightly wounding his horse and destroying the rations and vessels in the cookhouse. The Captain yelled, "Ammunition orderly wanted," and I volunteered. I jumped on the horse, galloped him as well as his limping leg would permit, and weathered the storm of shells through the fire zone, making my way to the wagon lines, where I gave the Quartermaster the order.

Then I had the pleasure of witnessing for the first time the admirable celerity and effectiveness with which an order of this kind is carried out.

"Ten loads of ammunition wanted at once, sir; ammunition pretty nearly exhausted at the guns," was the message I delivered. The Quartermaster blew his whistle—"Stand to! ammunition up!" he yelled. The Sergeant then carried on; the men were standing easy by their horses waiting for the word. In these days, when a battle is on, the men are always ready for the word at a moment's notice, with their horses fully harnessed, nothing being removed from the animals except the bit to enable them to take their feed from the bag, and in no case is an ammunition wagon left without its guard; at night when the guard would lie down to snatch an hour's sleep, another one was there ready to carry on. "Prepare to mount! Mount! Walk—march! Trot!" yelled the Sergeant in quick succession, each command being executed with clock-like exactness, and they trotted from under cover of the trees where they were concealed from the airplanes and proceeded rapidly up the road under shell fire, bumping and stumbling along.

I was guide for the party. We passed through Breeland, but could not make the best kind of speed as the traffic was terribly congested. On the left hand side of the road long lines of ambulances bearing wounded men were going down, stretcher bearers were carrying their suffering burdens and wounded men who were able to walk were making their way around and through the wagons as best they could, among them being men from every branch of the Imperial service, together with French and Algerians; on the other side of the road supply wagons of all descriptions were going forward. In the course of our journey the harness of one of the horses rubbed the animal until he was lame, stopping up the wagon. Immediately the Sergeant who was riding alongside ordered the wagon to one side, removed the horse, installed his own, jumped on the wagon and caught up with the others. The speed with which he did the trick almost made me gasp with astonishment; in all my life I never saw work of the kind handled so smoothly and swiftly. A dash of the picturesque was added to the scene by the Algerian ration-bearers winding their way in and out of the wagons, carrying trays of hot food on their heads and shoulders. It was nothing short of marvelous, the skillful manner in which they carried their precious burden of food, for never did they have a spill unless killed or wounded.

One of the funniest sights a man can see was the way my chums of the ammunition wagons defied the explicit and peremptory order,

S.O.S. Stand to!

"No smoking on the road at or around Ypres." There is something in the rise and fall of the lighted cigarette when being smoked that attracts the attention at long distances and many a man has had to pay the penalty, which was most severe,—28 days field punishment, which means 28 days without pay and breaking your back at fatigue duty around the camp, the cookhouse and the wagon lines, in addition to four hours extra drill each day. The temptation to smoke is so compelling that the punishment does not deter most men and they take the chance. By taking the collar of their coat and tucking it around their faces, lighting the match under their coat next to their ribs, burying their faces in their coat, they get a light without much danger of detection. In puffing it a man will hold the fag in his closed fist to his mouth, take the inhale, and, if there should happen to be a provo or other suspicious guardian of the rules in sight, down into his stomach would go the smoke. I don't know why it is but it has always seemed to me that the more stringent the rules are against the forbidden luxury, the more chances men will take to get their smoke.

We made the run to Ypres Square in an hour and a half. As soon as we entered I noticed a woman clinging tightly to a little girl and hugging the wall of the Nunshouse, a building standing immediately opposite the town hall in the square. The square itself was a large open place in the city about 350 feet long by 150 wide. I jumped off my horse, gave it to the driver and went over. In broken English I learned they wanted to cross, but on account of the fire continually bursting the woman would not, so I picked up the child and carried her across to a cellar about five doors out of the square. A chunk had been blown out of the building and there was no difficulty in getting into the cellar, and as soon as I got to this place the child murmured, "*Bon! bon!*" and indicated she would go in there. I set her down and she turned her pretty little face to me for a kiss. She then caught my arm as I was about to go and slipping off a tiny locket from her little neck, handed it to me, indicating that she wanted me to keep it. I have it to this day and I prize it tenderly. It has a small picture of the patron saint of France, Joan of Arc.

I ran back to her mother, pointed out where the child was, but she still seemed afraid to venture across. Although my little adventure did not occupy over three minutes, I could wait no longer, and jumped on my horse and the train of wagons trotted sharply out of the square. As the last wagon was leaving, I heard a sound like a train leaving a depot—choo! choo! choo! choo! growing louder each instant, and as the tail-end of the last wagon was trotting out of the square a shell, the largest ever employed by the German command and called the Ypres Express, landed full in the square, killing every living thing there and destroying ambulances and wagons of every kind, catching our rear wagon and blowing it up, wounding the driver and destroying the magnificent Cloth Hall, the last vestige of this most beautiful piece of architecture being destroyed by the resulting fire. That shell was from one of two guns that were expressly manufactured for the purpose of destroying the city of Ypres, a couple of months being taken to build cement platforms in which to set the ordnance, and the death-dealing monsters started on their mission of destruction from Dixmude, about 22 miles distant.

British Battery in Action

Not long after, an airplane located these monsters and succeeded in destroying one by a downpour of explosives he dropped on it, and the other one, a couple of days following, when being fired by its crew, the shell exploded in the gun itself, tearing it from its cement foundation and destroying itself and crew. These were the only guns of that caliber that have ever been used, so far as is known. The passage through the air of those missiles of death, heralded by their choo! choo! sent a shiver of dread up and down the lines as far as the

S.O.S. Stand to!

sound would reach, and deep and lasting was the satisfaction of all ranks when the last of these mammoths of destruction wended its final flight.

CHAPTER V.
HUN HELPERS

On the sixth day after the first gas attack on the Canadians at Ypres, we took up a new position in a hedge about three-quarters of a mile north and a quarter of a mile east of Ypres, and about a thousand yards from the German trenches. We galloped like mad over the shell-swept road, taking just exactly an hour and a half to get the guns placed and blazing. We had four guns when we pulled into this position, but were latterly reinforced by two more from another battery, their sisters having been smashed and the crews bayoneted, including their commanding officers, and like friendless children they came to us looking for a home and were gladly taken in, thus increasing our battery to six guns.

The hedge of the thickly growing thorn bushes ranged to the height of four feet, making it incumbent upon us to continually assume a stooping position when walking, involving a crick in the back for a good part of the time while there, but the bush was as thick as could be and formed an admirable shelter.

The beauty of these hedges in blossoming time is charming and the buds were now coming out, their fragrance filling the air with sweet nectar. To our right was a large farmhouse, of two stories and a gable roof, and the nearest gun to the house was not over 30 feet off. The house was occupied by a farmer, his wife and two young children, a boy and a girl.

The farmer's demeanor toward us was that of a systematic grouch and his appearance did not belie his disposition—as surly and sulky looking as a whipped criminal. He would stand in the doorway, watching us continually, as if he feared we were going to steal his house from over his head, and about the only thing he would say was to warn us not to destroy the hedge. But our love for the shelter, to say nothing of our love for the fragrant blossoms, made this injunction needless.

Over on the other side of the house, 40 feet to the right of it, was another hedge behind which was a French battery of .75's. This

S.O.S. Stand to!

battery had been through the Marne and they were veterans of the finest order, the very cream of the French artillery service, and their Captain was an educated gentleman, speaking English as fluently as his native tongue. They had come up from the Champagne district to reinforce the position at Ypres and their battery also consisted of six guns, each gun capable of 24 shells a minute.

In appearance these guns are the last in the world to give one the impression of supreme efficiency; when we saw them coming down the road we wondered what they could be and were amazed when informed that they were the famous .75's that had made the work of the French guns ring throughout the world; we couldn't at first bring ourselves to believe that these were the famous guns until we saw them at work, because there is nothing in the general aspect of the piece to make one think that they are any better, if as good, as our old field pieces.

The secret of these magnificent guns lies in the buffer and in the ability of the muzzle of the gun to cool off; after discharging 24 rounds they are just as ready to discharge another 24 as when they started, while in the case of our pieces we have to let them cool, and 15 or 18 per minute is the limit of our effort, because any more would cause them to jam from the heat. There is no gun on earth that can compare with the .75's.

Our ammunition was supplied to us at this spot over a road running between our wagon lines, half way between Flamingad and Breevland, about a thousand yards away, but they had to go in a roundabout way, traveling fully 800 yards out of the direct route on account of the ditches. It was a physical impossibility for the horses to bring up sufficient ammunition for the guns during the night, and they had to make the perilous trip many times during the day, and with the German shells pounding the road every foot of the way, their fire being guided by the wireless directions from their planes, the number of horses that had their lives smashed out on this road was something enormous. At one spot is the famous Hell's Corner, so named because of the fierce fire that continually rained upon it, and here I counted 40 dead horses, as fine looking animals as ever were harnessed. Such is the toll of war.

S.O.S. Stand to!

On the day that we arrived, our attention was drawn to an Algerian who seemed to be an inmate of the house. He could speak some English and seemed to spend most of his time cleaning his revolver. On the first afternoon I asked him why he was there and to what regiment he belonged.

"The Algerian-African troop."

"I understood they were in the trenches," I said. "Are you with the infantry?"

"Yes," he replied, "I am."

"Are you wounded?"

"No."

"Then why are you not with your men?" I insisted.

"I was lost in the retreat," he answered.

"Why don't you go and look them up?"

"I did, but I can't find them."

Then he asked me if we were getting ammunition up.

"Oh, yes, lots of it," I said.

"When are you going to fire?"

"Oh, pretty soon," I said.

"What are you going to shoot at?" he asked.

I told him we were going to plug the German trenches and the buildings around there, that we had orders to blow them up as they were filled with machine guns. He grinned from ear to ear, saying, "Good! Good! Shoot them all! Which ones you shoot first? I want to see them fall."

I pointed out the ones my battery was going to demolish and his big white teeth were exposed in another grin, as he nodded approvingly, and walked off.

S.O.S. Stand to!

That same afternoon my gun leveled the buildings assigned to me for demolishment and knowing beyond all shadow of a doubt that they were filled with men and machine guns, I watched through the glasses to see the gray-clad inmates popping out of the doors and windows. Judge of my astonishment! Not a solitary soul left the building my gun had destroyed. I watched each one of them in turn and in turn was awarded nothing for my pains. From others, however, hundreds of men rushed and as they scurried away our guns shrapneled them, dropping them by the score.

A sort of a subconscious connection between my conversation with the Algerian and the effect of my gun fire found lodging in the back of my head, but it was not until later that it became a direct consciousness. Another thing that set me thinking was what seemed to me to be an undue familiarity between this Algerian trooper and our farmer; he had the entree of the house, apparently could go and come as he pleased, drinking coffee with the inmates, sleeping there nights and making himself generally at home. I didn't think much of it at the time, but later events made these trivialities very significant indeed.

The bombardment was now commencing to have its effect on me, and McLean and I were both tired out; we were dead beat and looked around for a quiet spot where we could rest. Billy McLean was my especial pal ever since I had set foot in France.

"Here is what the doctor ordered," he said, as we went off down the hedge a bit and came to a little opening in the bush into which we both crawled. It requires no effort for a man who has been sustaining the sound, shock and work of a bombardment, to fall asleep anywhere, any time, and we were soon Murphyized, as Mac expressed it.

The rain now commenced falling heavily and in the midst of our slumbers, an orderly happened along and woke me up. I gave Mac a shove and he too woke up. We were drenched and made for the barn. We found the Old Man there with a lantern and told him we were going up in the loft, but he scowled and said we were not to go. "To hell with you!"—and up we went, finding five or six of the boys there taking advantage of the lull to snatch an hour's sleep. We

S.O.S. Stand to!

quickly followed suit, getting hold of some straw and grain bags for a bed, and resumed our interrupted slumbers.

In the midst of our dreams "S.O.S. Stand to!" was ordered, but we did not hear. One of our fellows, as we later learned, came running up to the farmhouse and asked the farmer if he had seen any of our men.

"No," he scowled, "there are none here."

When we had our sleep out we made for the guns. It did not take us long to see that a pretty thorough strafing had been going on, yet so dead beat to the utter exhaustion point were we, that we had failed to hear them.

"Where the hell were you fellows?" asked one.

"Asleep up there in the barn," said I; "why didn't you call us?"

"I did, I asked that old blankety-blank and he told me he hadn't seen any of you fellows around there."

"Well," said I, "he knew that Mac and I were up there, because we told him we were going, although he didn't want to let us go."

Here the incident dropped and was forgotten for the time. That afternoon Fritz attempted to come over our way and on a "Stand to" we jumped to the guns and drove him back, sending across 200 expressions of our good will in record time. Then we "stood down." Following this we went through the usual routine of cleaning up our pet and making her ready for the next visitation, and while working away, friend farmer came along with one of his cows, a large white animal, leading it with a rope and permitting her to graze. He walked along in front of my gun where it stopped and grazed awhile; going in like manner in front of each of the guns. Then he led the animal over to the other side of the house, where it grazed in front of the French .75's.

In the meantime we were working hard, getting our pets in shape, and someone asked who would volunteer for water. We were all dirty, thirsty, greasy and tired, and I offered to go. I ambled over to

S.O.S. Stand to!

the farmhouse, stopping to speak to the Captain for a moment on the way, when I heard a shell explode; it had demolished No. 2 gun.

"Stand to!" yelled the Captain; then to the farmer, "Take that damned cow away." He hurried the cow off and put it in the barn, but he had no sooner gone than Kr-kr-kr-p! Kr-kr-kr-p! and the Captain and I were knocked off our feet. The water bottle was broken and I did not take time to get another but made for the guns. They were hammering our batteries thoroughly now and I was told to take shelter. I ran over to the farmhouse and asked the farmer's wife for a cup of coffee,—to sell me a cup, which she refused; in fact, her husband would not permit any of us to enter the house again. Then a smothering fire smashed the French battery, the destruction being so accurate and complete that it was done while I was asking and being refused the coffee! Just leaving the house, I met one of the French captains. "Did you notice anything peculiar in the farmer's actions?" he asked me; "I mean, with his white cow?"

"I told him I hadn't noticed anything peculiar, that I had noticed he had taken his white cow out in front of our battery, grazing her there just before the battery was shot up.

"Did the cow stop in front of your gun?"

"Yes, it stopped before each one of them."

"So it did at ours," he said.

"*Merci* Monsieur, you will hear from this." And he left in a hurry. He phoned the gendarmes in the city of Ypres and in less than half-an-hour they came. They entered the farmhouse and searched it thoroughly. Upstairs they found parts of a heliograph lamp and a complete telephone apparatus; there was also in his stove a system that had been inaugurated for forcing up a shower of sparks; this apparatus had been found in the houses of a number of spies who had paid the penalty for their work. Then they made a search of the cellar in which were found hundreds of tins of beef and jam, all of which had come from our rations, and then was explained the mysterious disappearance of our grub. There was no trace to be found of our Algerian trooper; he had made a hasty exit.

S.O.S. Stand to!

Friend farmer and his wife were arrested, taken away with the children and placed in the coop, and there the traitorous couple got their deserts—they were taken to the square and shot.

After they had gone we made ourselves at home in the building, and the comforts that awaited us there made us feel almost glad that they had turned out to be spies. Among the rations we found that they had taken stuff that had been purloined from other units as far back as three months before. After a thorough ransacking and a feed that filled us to our heart's content, we made for the battery, being greeted with a fresh outburst on our arrival, and under the fire we pulled our remaining guns away to another hedge 200 yards off, and waited for the storm to settle.

While lying there the brains of one of our geniuses got to working and his ideas were quickly resolved into action. We went down to the barn, took a couple of wagons, taking off the wheels and the poles, and made up three dummy guns and placed them in the spot we had left, and in a few minutes' time we had the satisfaction of seeing Fritz spend three or four hundred good shells on our dummy battery.

A consuming thirst was parching my mouth and I took a chance and ran along the open to the house for a drink. Then it was that the disadvantageous side of our good work with the dummy guns was exemplified; just as I was stepping out of the door, a shell tore a hole in one corner of the building, knocking it out as clean as if it had been drilled.

The customary methods employed by the Germans to get information as to our guns, our troops, our supplies around Ypres, was to send a disguised soldier to the different farmhouses and threaten them with instant demolition by their guns if they did not furnish the information sought for, and thus did Fritz make good his promise to the farmer. By reason of our dummy guns and the strafing they got, and the fact that our guns still were firing, he believed that the farmer had given him a bunco steer, and he lost no time in making good his word.

S.O.S. Stand to!

Remaining in the hedge for a few hours, we dug holes for the guns, covered them with tarpaulins and grass on top, giving them the usual scenic shelter. We did this work in the open but only one man at a time exposed; it was as much as life was worth for more than one to be seen working. That evening, in the midst of our meal at cookhouse,—"Stand to!" and we raced for our pets. When the concert was well under way, Munsey noticed a light three or four hundred yards off that was acting somewhat peculiarly; it would flare up and down oddly and seemed to be in a farmhouse straight at our rear, but not much attention was paid to it at the time. Next morning Munsey and I were in the cookhouse, trying to moisten a couple of hardtack biscuits with what juice we could extract from a piece of bacon rind, when an airplane hummed overhead and the attention of one of our anti-aircraft guns was immediately diverted to the bird. The cookhouse had formerly been a French dressing station, dismantled by the fire of those devils that know no law of God or man, composed of three huts in a row made of half-inch board. While eating, one of our own shells, a shrapnel, that had been sent up at a German stork and did not explode, dropped squarely into the middle of the cookhouse, frightened the cook out of his wits and hit the dixies, scattering them around our feet. "Stand to!" and we made our way carefully, keeping out of sight as much as possible from the watching bird overhead.

When I got to the gun the shell fire was commencing to get dangerously close. "By God, there must be somebody giving our battery away," said Munsey. A number of our men had been wounded at this time and the airplane still buzzing above, made it impossible for us to fire, and we got a "Stand down!"

"Come on over," Munsey proposed, "and we'll see what's in that building where I saw the light." We found a family of civilians living there and they were at once very solicitous about giving us coffee. "Never mind the coffee," said Munsey; "we have come to examine the house." The old man seemed quite willing to have us do so and pointed the way upstairs, starting himself to go out the door. Munsey grabbed him by the arm,—"Come along and show us the way." He indicated that we could find the way ourselves, but my mate was insistent and he forced the old man along and upstairs we went.

At first nothing resulted from our thorough search, but Munsey's eye lighted on an Algerian serge lying in the corner of the room, and almost at the same time I noticed some bricks in the chimney that seemed to be loose. An old table in the middle of the room I pulled over to the chimney, tugged at some of the brick that I had noticed, and the whole thing caved in, part of a heliograph outfit falling out. The old fellow made a dart for the door, but was peremptorily intercepted. "Damn you, stay where you are!" I pulled out the rest of the stuff; there was a complete heliograph apparatus, and a little red cap, such as the Algerians wear, satisfying us both that the man doing the work used the uniform of an Algerian.

On leaving the room, carrying the stuff with us and going down stairs, we saw a box against the wall and I heard a funny noise from it as if it contained something alive. I pulled it out and found it full of pigeons. "Who owns these?" I asked.

"An Algerian soldier left them there," he answered.

We then examined the cellar and entire basement, but found nothing further. We took the old fellow over to the gendarme who immediately took charge of him, and returned to the battery where we imparted the news of our find. It was the consensus of opinion that the spy was the farmer himself, and that the Algerian uniform was a blind. We were chatting away, discussing the matter, when the shells commenced flying as thick as peas in a pod; so swift and smashing was the fusillade that for awhile I thought hell's gate had opened wide. In less than no time one of our guns was knocked out and, getting a "Stand to!" we replied as fast as our legs and arms and heads would work.

The excellent quality of the work that Fritz did here made the fellows unanimous that his information came from the farmer. Presently the duel cooled down and we resumed our chat.

About a hundred yards off from the farmhouse where we had found the heliograph and Algerian uniform, was a windmill of the kind

S.O.S. Stand to!

commonly seen in the farmhouses of the country, with large wings, and it happened that while firing, one of the boys, Boxer, noticed that the mill was going around in an irregular fashion,—going first one way and then another, and then stopping, and he called our attention to it and we all noticed it, and almost simultaneously with our observation of the mill, four shells came over, knocking another of our guns into uselessness and wiping out the crew, and after we got "Stand down!" and had cleaned up, Boxer suggested that we go over and see what was in the windmill.

Together we went, going first to the house, and found the children crying with fright; some of them tried to tell us something, but we couldn't make out what they were saying. We crossed over to the windmill and a phenomenon indeed met our eyes,—the wheel was turning in the opposite direction from that in which the wind was blowing. We started up the steps and—Ping! Ping! and Boxer fell with an oath and a bullet in his leg. I assisted him to the farmhouse and then scooted over and communicated with the O.C. I also informed a French battery that had been terrifically shelled.

In the meantime a stretcher had been sent for, and Boxer was brought back to the dressing station, where he had his wound dressed, which luckily turned out to be slight.

That night I was filled full of the spirit of adventure and I wanted to visit the windmill again. I got a pal to go with me and endeavored to make it, but the flares were steadily burning and the snipers were so busy we had to lie low. Again I went to the French battery and told the officer commanding of my suspicions about the windmill. A smile of intelligence and gratefulness lighted up his fine face. "Monsieur, we shall see what we shall see," and he ordered a shell into the heart of the structure, bringing it down in splinters. Then we made for the ruins and found the body of a man dressed in an Algerian uniform; I looked him over carefully; he was the artist I had met in the farmhouse at our former station.

There remained still the case of the old man in whose house we had discovered the heliograph and the pigeons. And the gendarmes were again sent for and the Belgian farmer was haled before the officer. With white face and streaming eyes he told the French Captain of the

S.O.S. Stand to!

gendarmes that this man had come to him and told him that if he didn't permit him to go into his home, he would instantly signal for the shells and he and his family and buildings would be blown to eternity. The old man was permitted to go, as the French officer was satisfied he was sincere, but that he was utterly powerless to prevent the spy carrying out his plans.

In conversation with us later, the farmer told us that the Algerian had brought pigeons with him; that he had written notes, put them in the little cup fastened to the bird's foot and sent some of them off, the others remaining in the box when the Algerian went upstairs. "I could hear the bricks falling, but he called to us not to come upstairs," went on the old man. "Shortly afterwards a man dressed in the uniform of a British soldier came, and he too went upstairs; he was carrying a bag. When he came in he asked if I wanted coffee and I answered 'No.' When he came in the Algerian called down to send him up, and he too went up. Presently the British soldier left and a few minutes afterwards your battery started firing. Then out ran the Algerian, saying he was going to the windmill and warned all of us on pain of losing our lives, not to come near the mill. That is the last I saw of him, Messieurs, until this evening when I see his dead body.

"I am heart and soul with you, Messieurs; I know what you are doing for us and for Belgium; but you can see that I had no chance whatever to communicate with you; my life would have been the price, and what would have become of my family? If there had been anything I could have done, Messieurs, I would most gladly have done it, but I couldn't do anything, and the spy would have accomplished his purpose just the same had I made an attempt."

It was now about 6:30 and on our way back to the gun pit we met a woman who seemed to be in the depths of despair, accompanied by a little girl. The woman was weeping bitterly. Our nerves were on edge and we were suspicious of everybody; trickery, deceit, traitor-work seemed to be in the very air itself, and we made a resolve that we would shoot anybody, man, woman or child, whom we saw loitering around our guns who had no business there; that very day the O.C. had sworn that he would ask no questions, but would shoot on sight. The woman's story was pitiful in the extreme.

S.O.S. Stand to!

"Oh, what shall I do, what shall I do! My home is gone! My husband is gone! My children are gone! And for what?"—wringing her hands and gesticulating wildly. "For what, Messieurs? For being quiet, inoffensive, loyal people!"

In my clumsy fashion I succeeded in somewhat calming the poor creature, and she proceeded a little more coherently.

"Well, Messieurs, a man in Algerian uniform came to our house this morning. He asked permission of my husband, who was a loyal Belgian, to use our house—for what? To do spy work. My husband ran for a gun and warned him off. He said, 'You had better think it over; if you don't let me use your house you have not another day to live!' In spite of this, my husband presented the gun at him and he made off, but as he was leaving he called back, 'Do not on any account leave the house today, any of you, or you will be killed.'

"We watched him and saw him go towards the hedge, and two or three men with bags met him, and they made off in the direction of your battery. Then, then—*Mon Dieu!* How can I tell it!—a shell came and destroyed our home, killing my dear husband and my two babies."

And again the poor woman burst into a paroxysm of weeping and sank to the ground in an utterly exhausted condition, moaning aloud in the despair of her misery. Her little daughter was screaming in terror at the plight of her mother, and we all set about to comfort them as best we could, but ah! God! how comfortless our words.

The thought that perhaps the child would be quieted if she had something to eat suggested itself to me, but I had nothing except my iron rations, and our orders are very stern that under no circumstances must these be consumed except at the time designated, namely, when our supply wagons are destroyed and cannot reach us, and the order is issued from headquarters that we may use them. These rations are 16 ounces of bully beef, two hardtack biscuits, some tea and sugar in small wax envelopes. Each man must carry his own iron rations at all times and the penalty for eating them without orders is 28 to 90 days, first field punishment; therefore, I was taking a chance, but I hadn't the heart to resist the pitiful wail of that kiddie, and I felt that the risk I took was amply repaid by the cessation of her childish grief. The mother also had had nothing to eat all day, and she partook of some of the nourishment and was the better for it.

There was nothing more for them that we could do and they departed, the poor creature with an expression in her eyes that plainly said, she didn't know where on earth she was going, and cared less.

This was only an individual instance of the tens of thousands of blasted and stricken homes and families, resulting from the rule or ruin policy of the German "man of God."

Half an hour after they had departed a train of ammunition wagons came galloping up, the driver telling us that in passing Hell's Corner they were given an exceptionally heavy dose by Fritz. "His aim the nicht was damn puir, however," said one of the Scotch drivers; "he never gave us a scratch; but I noticed on the road a woman wi' a little bairn, a wee thing, hardly higher than your knee, and as we were racing by them, a shell exploded on the side of the road, right alongside o' them, blawin' the puir things to their doom."

From the description furnished by the driver, I was convinced it was the poor woman and child for whom I had taken the risk of punishment, and I could not help thinking what a blessing it was that death had come to them in the way it did, so soon after her inextinguishable sorrow.

Another evidence testamentary of the industry of the German agents came to us that very night from the driver. After the wagons were loaded up at the wagon lines, someone undid the locks of the wagons and on the way to the guns the shells dropped out from time to time, scattering over the cobble stones, causing them to lose more than half of their precious loads.

"Aye," said the Scotch driver who had told us about the woman and her child, "and a French battery coming up behind us, the horse kicked one shell that we dropped, and I'm damned if it did na'

S.O.S. Stand to!

explode and blaw the puir beggars to the deil. By the Lord! They're doing gude work!" Good work, indeed, Fritz, but your day is coming!

Next morning about ten o'clock we got a "Stand to!" as a bombardment had begun and Fritz had started coming over. We stopped him, but no sooner had we ceased firing than Kr-kr-kr-p! Kr-kr-kr-p! Bang! Bang! coming down so fast that we made off for shelter at the cookhouse. While there, Munsey thought he would like to have a look at the situation generally in the surrounding country, through the medium of a hole in the side of the cookhouse up near the roof and he hopped on top of a box and looked out in the direction of Ypres. The most notable object there was the town clock, and he had not been looking long before he noticed the hands moving this way and that; he watched closely and then called, "Come here, fellows, quick. Come and watch the clock!" We all jumped to a point of vantage and watched, and in few minutes we were satisfied that the shell fire that was raining upon us was being directed by the hands of the clock. We observed that when the long hand moved right, the rain of fire would increase; when it moved left, it decreased; each jump of the hand five minutes meant 25 yards increase or decrease, as the case might be. Every time the small hand moved one minute right, it meant three yards right; two minutes, six yards, and so on; and the same if it veered to the left. And when both hands turned at once to 12:00 o'clock we deduced from their fire that some object was registered and when that was done the large hand would go all the way around and the fire would increase to a regular hurricane; if it went half way round, it would decrease. The small hand going all the way round, the fire ceased.

We watched intently for some time, keeping our eyes glued on the movement of the hands in conjunction with the fire, and then the matter was phoned to headquarters. A result of their combination guns and clockwork was the destruction of one of our pieces and two of the French battery. Another battery observer had noticed the clockwork at the same time that we were watching it, and the gendarmes were notified; they made a trip to the top of the tower in double quick time, finding there a man in a British uniform and one in French uniform; the man with the British uniform wore a French

S.O.S. Stand to!

cap and he in the French had a British cap. They were taken and confined in the basement of a ruined building and a guard set.

That night I was sent to the trench headquarters to do guard duty and next day, about 11:00 o'clock in the morning, I was standing in the doorway of the farmhouse where the pump had blown in on Scotty, and I was accosted by two men who were walking rapidly. They asked me where a certain Algerian Regiment was lying and I directed them, after giving them a drink of water and a biscuit. They also asked me what those headquarters were, and a number of other questions. However, no suspicion of there being anything wrong entered my mind, as they spoke perfect English. They left and had just turned the corner to cross a pontoon bridge over Yser Canal, going toward the front-line trenches, when three French guards came running like mad. They asked me some questions excitedly, but it was some time before I could make out what they wanted.

Finally I got it through my head and told them and they raced off. The men who had accosted me were the two prisoners who had been taken in the clock tower at Ypres, as I heard subsequently, but they did not get away with their nervy trick; they were taken and paid the price.

That same night a bunch of the 48th Highlanders, of Toronto, were on our right, and dug in in the bank, but there was considerable water in the bottom of their holes, while ours, compared to theirs, were beautifully dry. The Kilties came along, searching for blankets and whatever they could get, and we spared them whatever we could. Then one of them spotted a farmhouse, the occupants of which had been shelled out because they would not comply with the orders of a German agent, and had lost their home in consequence. They went in and helped themselves to straw and came out loaded down with armfuls of it. I decided to follow suit and went over, just reaching the barn, when Kr-kr-kr-p!—the first shell that came going right amongst them, setting the barn on fire and wounding several of the 48th. Their presence had been made known by a secret service agent, as it is one chance in a hundred thousand for a shell to hit so desirable a target at the first shot. The aim was excellent and the work accomplished by the shell was splendid—from a German point of view.

CHAPTER VI
BITS OF BATTLE

On the way over to the barn, where the shell hit the 48th, a piece of a tree limb smashed into the ground at my feet, following the familiar whiz just overhead of a large gun missive, with its accompanying wind gust, and at the same moment something struck with a thud the tree from which the splinter had come. Glancing up, I noticed a shell lodged in a fork of the two main branches, that had stuck there without exploding. For a shell to explode, it is necessary that the nose of the fuse, containing the detonator, shall come in contact with a solid substance, in order to make ignition and cause the explosion. This had not been done; owing to the intervention of kind nature in the shape of the crotch in that tree catching and holding the shell fast in a firm embrace, we were saved from that additional disaster and death.

A dried-up creek that was being used by us for a trench on the Ypres sector was crossed by a wooden bridge about thirty feet long. This bridge was used as a means of transport at night and by Red Cross men in the daytime, and was very useful; it was most important that it be kept in constant repair. I was detailed in charge of the repair party. One day during the great Ypres battle, about ten o'clock in the morning, the bridge was smashed and I took my party up and made the necessary repairs. We had hardly returned to cover when the bridge was smashed again, and again we rushed out and fixed it up. As we ran, three men forged ahead of me and got to the middle of the thirty-foot structure; I was about twenty feet behind them, the rest of the party immediately behind me. I was shouting an order to them, when a shell exploded in the middle of the bridge, killing all three. I was saved by twenty feet.

In the late afternoon one day of the battle, I was resting in a hole I had burrowed under a sand-bank; about 200 men were burrowed in the same bank in the same way. A monster shell struck the bank immediately above me, upheaving the ground and completely burying me and half a dozen others. I was dug out in a half smothered condition, but soon was able to assist in the work of resurrecting the rest. The only casualty that occurred in that incident was innocently caused by myself; as I was digging, my shovel struck the leg of an officer, inflicting such a gash that when resuscitated he had to go to hospital.

A cunning device of the Germans to misuse the Red Cross came to light during the next few days. It was in the vicinity of the woods where the Imperial Batteries had lost their guns. In a counter attack to retake these guns our men went over, accompanied by the engineers, to destroy the guns, as it was thought it would be impossible to bring them back. This turned out to be true, as the enemy advanced in such strong mass formation that our fellows had their hands full fighting them off until the engineers made good their work, which they did by smashing the hydraulic buffers with picks, destroying the sights, blowing the guns up, and taking the breech-blocks back with them.

In going over the ground that our barrage had covered a few minutes before, we found lying there German soldiers who had acted as stretcher bearers, wearing the red cross of Geneva on their arms, for the purpose of running wires from trench to trench, from battery to battery, and to headquarters, and the way they did the trick was to take a roll of wire on a stretcher covered with a blanket, to represent a wounded comrade, start the roll unwinding and running the wire between their legs as they walked. The blankets on the stretchers were used to deceive our observers and make them believe they were doing honest hospital work in the field. This was only one of their many unprincipled practices, for the Germans ignored all usages of war as practiced by civilization.

During the busiest days of May, 1915, between the second and third battle of Ypres, I was on guard duty at field headquarters in the trenches. The Staff was located in an old two-story building that was much the worse for wear from German calling cards. My "go" was from eight to ten P.M. Promptly at ten o'clock a rap came to the door and, blowing out the light, I inquired who it was. It was my relief, Dave Evans, one of the best pals whom it has ever been my lot to soldier with. Dave was a heavy-set man, strong as an ox; I think he could have almost felled a bull with his fist, so powerful was he. I re-

S.O.S. Stand to!

lit the candle after closing the door. This was Dave's first "go" at this particular spot, and I cautioned him to be careful not to show himself in the open doorway with the light behind him, as the building was under observation and the splinters that were being continually chipped from it demonstrated how keenly active and alert they were, and made it necessary for a man to be on the lookout every second of the time. He said he would take no chances. Dave had just obtained an Enfield rifle, for which he had been very glad to exchange his Ross, as the Enfield is better suited for trench purposes, and, not being thoroughly familiar with its workings, he asked me to explain it to him, which I did. Then I blew out the light, opened the door, whispered "good-night," and started down the path. About a hundred feet away I heard Dave calling me back; I turned; he was standing in the doorway, with the candle light gleaming behind him. He called out, "Grant, I don't quite get this safety catch and bolt; would you mind showing it to me again?"

"Blow out the light, you damn fool," I called.

"All right," and he did so and I started back. As he answered me I heard simultaneously the report of a rifle and the whiz of a bullet passing me. When I got to the door I stumbled over the body of my friend Dave; he had received the summons through the head.

While standing guard at the open door, before Dave came, with the light out, however, I suddenly got a start that frightened me more than anything else that has happened me in France: In the gleam of a distant flare, the white faces of two women peered around the corner of the building, looking at me through the open door. There was something so damnably uncanny in their appearance, and so startling, that a cold sweat broke out over me, and I snapped my rifle to the present. Had they not been women they would not have lived; a loiterer around headquarters takes his life in his hands.

They had been there that same afternoon, saying they were the owners of the place, and that they had stopped to take away some supplies. They were permitted to take their goods with them, but were warned against coming there again. They did not heed the warning. I reported their presence to the O.C. and they were promptly arrested and handed over to the French police. What their lot was I cannot tell, but to this day I can't help thinking that in some way poor Dave owes his fate to those women.

After two days' hard marching we reached Givenchy June 9, 1915, a little town in France lying thirty miles south of Ypres. Our battery of two guns took up its position immediately outside, on the southwest side of the town. A few civilians were scattered through the town, living in the cellars, the rest having fled at the German approach. We were ordered to put our guns in the very front-line trench for the reason that the opposing trenches being so close together, it was impossible for the guns to do justice to themselves without inflicting serious casualties on our own men. To make our work as noiseless as possible, we took a number of old rubber tires, cut them in strips and wrapped them around the gun wheels with hay wire; this facilitated both the movement of the guns and the preservation of silence.

We again had the honor of being the sacrifice battery for the division—in other words, having the profound pleasure of going heavenward, or in the other direction, before any of the others, for the purpose of working out the plan of action by the Command. We got the guns into position under cover of night, and thoroughly camouflaged them with grass and tree branches. We did the job so artistically that the birds would come and chatter and sing immediately over the guns when they were not telling their tale of love to Fritz.

Out in front of our guns was a small ridge or embankment, gradually sloping up to a height of twenty feet and extending east and west for a distance of three or four hundred yards. This rising piece of ground was a decided obstacle to our progress and it was ordered mined for the purpose of leveling it. The engineers attended to the task. It turned out that Fritz also had mined the ridge in order to blow our sector skyward.

The stage was set and the play started at 5:30 in the afternoon. Our orders were to blow holes in the parapet wire which ran in a zigzag direction every way out in front, for the purpose of enabling the infantry to get through when they got over. Our ammunition was of the best; we now took no chance on any defective goods. We had 20 rounds of shell for each gun. When we got the order—"Fire!" gaps

S.O.S. Stand to!

were torn in the wire by my gun, and the other gun had blown away some small ridges. We were going strong when a shell—the very first one—took our other gun, blowing it and the crew into nothingness. We went on firing until we had exploded 18 shells and had made several gaps in the wire, when, without a moment's warning, our trench mine exploded. The trenches were packed with troops ready for the word. A mountain of debris was shot in the air and back over us, burying a number of soldiers in the trench, where they died miserably from suffocation. The concussion was so powerful that it blew the shield of my gun off downwards, cleaving Corporal King's skull in twain and blowing Gunner MacDonald, who was sitting on the handspike of the gun, 20 feet away. When we found him next day, every bone in his body was broken. I was sitting on the gun alongside of Corporal King at the time of his death, and how I escaped is more than I can tell. Again I couldn't help speculating that my life must have been spared for some good purpose; I sincerely hope so.

It was impossible to do any further firing, as the muzzle of the gun was choked completely with the dirt that had been shot backward by the explosion of our own mine. Our misfortune, however, did not prevent or deter for a moment the intended movement. Unable to do anything further as a gunner, I hopped into the charge with the 48th Highlanders of Toronto, who had just started with one of their old-time yells to go out and over. When we reached the German front lines,—or what was left of them, for the explosion had blown from them all semblance of a trench,—it was jammed full of German troops—dead. On we went, inclining to the right and reaching an orchard in which was a nest of them concealed in the trees. Those on mother earth were speedily driven to hell or made good their escape, and we then attended to the case of the squirrels in the branches. This was somewhat difficult, as the night was excessively dark, but our snipers, circling everywhere underneath them, finally got them; not a single baby-killer escaped; it was a case of getting limburgers in an apple tree.

No sooner had we cleaned up the job than the Fritzies returned *en masse* formation, compelling us to beat a discretionary retreat to their front-line trenches, where we held and are still holding, and then some. Here we remained until the middle of the following month.

S.O.S. Stand to!

Some minor engagements took up my duties after Givenchy, until about September 1, when my battery was instructed to proceed to Ploegsteert.

Ploegsteert sets in ruins about two miles northwest of Armentières; there were no buildings that Fritz failed to level with the exception of the tower, which they used for registry purposes,—a reference point in artillery technology. We were stationed on this sector for eight months, and our stay here was more or less of a recreation; battle firing was only intermittent; and on the days that we did speak to Fritz, we rarely sent over more than 10 to 12 messages.

Our battery was in a hedge here and we were having our wires cut several times, causing us considerable trouble and annoyance.

Butler, one of my pals, was started out to make the necessary repairs. He left on his dangerous mission, crouching along and taking advantage of every bit of shelter on the way, but several ping! pings! warned him that he was treading on danger ground. He kept at his work, busily hunting for the break in the wire, with the sniping pills passing his ears continually.

Crawling along on his hands and knees, with the wire running through his hand, he came to a little bush, where it slipped away from him, denoting that there was the break. At that moment the sniper got him in the leg, but he held to until he repaired it, and was in touch with headquarters, reporting that he had mended the break, when the wire was again cut. The bleeding from his wound now made it necessary for him to mend that break first, and he bandaged it as quickly as his nervous fingers would work. Again he took hold of the wire, crawling and stumbling along until he again came to the break, and again mended it. He was being closely watched now, as the bullets were whistling about him ceaselessly. Again he turned his attention to his wound, adjusting the bandage, and he noticed a British soldier crawling toward him on his hands and knees.

"Hello, matey, what you doing out here?" he asked.

"I'm mendin' me bloomin' leg now," Butler answered.

S.O.S. Stand to!

"Well, if you hadn't been out here you wouldn't have got it. Why didn't you stay in your trenches?"

"Someone's got to repair the wire," said Butler. He was growing perceptibly weaker from the loss of blood.

"Oh, repairing the wire, were you? Well, don't repair any more"—and Butler had just time to see him level his revolver and then he dropped unconscious. The bullet had hit him in the thigh. But his communication had reached headquarters that he was wounded and it was not long before the stretcher bearers came out and found him. They took him to the dressing station, where it was found necessary to amputate his leg, but he parted gladly with his dented member when the O.C. told him that his grit and endurance were a splendid example for the entire unit,—"Aye," he added, "and for the whole Empire."

Service was being held here in the field one Sunday morning and an incident occurred that makes me shake every time I think of it,—not so much at the incident itself as in the surrounding circumstances. In the midst of the service, a buzzing overhead announced the presence of German hawks and a dropping of bombs further announced that they had seen us and intended paying their respects.

A face turned upward is one of the most easily detected objects by an airplane, and although we had strict orders on no account to look up, the temptation for some was too strong. Meantime, the minister continued to read the service, but the responses were not as hearty as they had been, and he himself was standing with shoulders hunched up to the back of his neck, the book pulled up to his nose, and furtively trying to see through his eyebrows the danger-birds in the blue. In the midst of the solemn moment an officer, glimpsing some of the men turning their faces skyward, bellowed, "Damn you, keep those mugs down."

It was our good fortune that none of the messages reached their intended destination.

S.O.S. Stand to!

CHAPTER VII
SANCTUARY WOODS

(3rd Battle of Ypres)

The third battle of Ypres commenced June 2, lasting until June 15, 1916. Sanctuary Woods was a cluster of trees, comprising about one thousand in number, and they were the very finest and noblest specimens of their various types,—oak, elm, ash and beech. They were located just one mile outside the city in a northwesterly direction. One of our trenches ran northeast and southwest through the middle of the woods.

The line had been exceptionally quiet for the space of a week. My battery of six guns was located at a château known as the Belgian Garden, about 600 yards in the rear of the wood. Two guns were ordered into the wood as a sacrifice battery, and my usual luck attached me to one of them. We were located in a dry ditch, 300 yards back from the front line. Our orders, as usual in the case of the sacrifice battery, were to wait until the Germans, when they broke through, if they did, were almost in line with our guns.

The morning of the 2nd was a beautiful summer's day; nature was in perfect repose; the birds sang gayly, the humming of bees and fragrance of flowers filled the air. We were busily engaged making our morning ablutions in some shell holes when, like a bolt from the blue, hell broke loose in the form of the most violent bombardment I had experienced up to that time, lasting twenty minutes, missiles of every kind raining down on us on all sides. "Stand to!"—and we waited.

At the end of twenty minutes our men started jumping out of their trenches ahead of us and charging across. They were met by the enemy in mass formation and overwhelmed. They died to a man. The Germans pressed the attack home and came on, yelling like fiends incarnate, drunk with the joy of their apparent success and promised victory. On they came, apparently irresistible. We commenced firing, and I had the satisfaction of seeing gaps blown in their ranks and many of them biting the dust. Our poor little battery, however, feazed them but little.

And I want to say right at this time that the idea that seems to be prevalent in the minds of many that the German is not a good fighting man is a lamentable mistake; he is a good fighter. He has not perhaps the initiative of the British, or the avalanche-like ardor in a charge of the French soldier, but with his officers pressing him behind and in mass formation, he is as formidable a foe as can be imagined.

Our ammunition was exhausted, not a shell remaining, and we grabbed our rifles, retreating with the rest, and sniping and dropping as we fell back. We took parts of the guns with us to prevent Fritz making use of it, and threw them into a shell hole filled with water, as they were too heavy to carry and manipulate our rifles at the same time, and that ability was much more precious to us at that particular time than the gun-parts. One of my chums had been wounded in the pit before we retired, and was later taken prisoner, and two of my other chums were killed in the general retreat. My pals with the other guns, forty feet to our right, did not get all of their ammunition off before the Boches were upon them, and they, too, died there; they were incinerated alive in their little pit by smoke shells that started everything ablaze as they exploded.

The retreat ended in Maple Copse Woods, where we established ourselves and held the Germans, they resting at the edge of Sanctuary Woods. Under orders, I and my partner started for Zillebeke, about 400 yards back from Maple Copse, where we established an observation station, with the necessary telephonic communication to headquarters, which, when done, was taken in charge by a relief party from another battery, and I returned to Belgian Gardens at 11:30 A.M., where I was put in charge of another gun crew.

I thought I had done a fairly good morning's work and was hoping Fritz would behave himself for the balance of the day, but my hope was a delusion, for inside of half an hour Fritzie thought he would like to see the scenery in Maple Copse, and came on for another try. Heavy firing began, lasting about five minutes, and over they came again. We opened up heavily with our battery of four guns, throwing a barrage in his front as best we could; mine was the only battery left working on this particular sector. Our fellows went out and met Fritz in a hand-to-hand argument, backing up their contention so thoroughly with the cold steel that they sent him flying back to the line he had established at Sanctuary Woods.

But it was necessary, in order to keep him quiet, to keep up a barrage. Our ammunition had run down to a point where we had only fourteen shells left, and we received orders to hold two high explosive shells, one for the muzzle and another for the breech of the gun, to put it out of business in case they broke through.

If it became necessary to resort to the expedient of blowing up the gun, it would be done by placing a shell in the breech of the chamber, the breech closed, another shell inside the muzzle, the lanyard fastened to the firing lever and strung out of the front pit door for a distance of 25 or 30 feet to a large tree standing at our rear, fastened to the tree, and when retreating pull it from there, blowing the gun and the gun pit into as many pieces.

Over the Top

We took all precautions when it became likely that we were going to be overpowered and there was a chance of Fritz taking our gun. It is rarely necessary to take this precaution nowadays, nor has it been for the last two years; the shoe is on the other foot now and the returns

S.O.S. Stand to!

showing the number of heavy German guns that we have captured within the last two years and a half, together with the fact that not a single British gun has been lost, shows how well the work is in hand on the Western Front.

With their unexcelled means of observation, they soon discovered where our little battery was hidden, and decided to end the argument with our troublemaker there and then.

A smothering fire burst upon us, and one of the shells clipped a large tree as easily as if it had been done with a giant razor, and it crashed down directly in front of our gun, putting it out of business for the time being.

In a few minutes more another shell landed on the gun forty feet to our left, ending its usefulness, killing the crew to a man and leaving but two guns working; a few moments more and another lit in the telephonists' pit fifteen feet to our rear, wiping out three or four of the fellows on duty there. Lord! it was getting hot!

We were then ordered to "Stand Down" (take cover), as the fire was getting hotter each second and it had all the appearance of being a wipe-out. I ordered my crew to beat it for the dugout, staying behind a moment or two to set the sight and fasten the lanyard to blow up the gun if needed. They started out of the gun pit, taking the turn to the right, along the path to the dugout, which was fairly well sheltered by big trees. I finished my work in a minute or two and took the turn to the left. When I reached the dugout the O.C. inquired where the men were.

"They ought to be here, sir; they left ahead of me. I will go at once and find them."

"I'll go with you." And we started through the trees. The dugout was only about forty yards in the rear of the gun pit and half way there we came across my crew lying underneath a huge tree, dead. It had been rooted from the ground, hurled in the air with the same ease as a toy balloon and dropped on the men. The hole torn in the ground at the root was big enough to swallow a horse and cart. Of the five members of my crew four were dead; the remaining man,

S.O.S. Stand to!

Bill Clark, had fourteen wounds in one side of his body from splinters of the tree.

I took him to the dressing station, where his wounds were dressed. As soon as he recovered consciousness he asked what had happened, and when I told him that his pals, including his bosom chum, Jim Chandler, had all been killed, he again lapsed into unconsciousness. He was later taken to the hospital, where, after a nine-months' battle with the Grim Reaper hovering constantly over his bed, he at last regained some of his old-time health. But he will never again be on the firing line.

Every man was now weary, sore and thirsty, and my only grateful recollection of that day's work was the O.C.'s command that we be given an extra ration of rum. I am not a constitutional advocate of the brew that glistens like gold, but that was one time when I thanked the good Lord for that drink.

Information was conveyed to the wagon lines of the terrible toll that had been exacted that day and the number of men that were needed to replace the casualties. Our parson, hearing what was going on in front, volunteered to come and officiate at the burial of the men that night, and mounting his horse he started in company with Archie Meehan and a small relief party.

In the meantime I had made my way back to the cellar of the château, which we were using for a dugout, and the battery to our rear, an Imperial battery, was firing when it received an "S.O.S." Suddenly a German airplane hovered over the château, describing a half circle behind the Imperial battery, spotting its flash, and immediately wirelessing the location. Our observers, who were stationed at points on either side, did not notice the manipulation of the airplane at the rear of the battery. The "S.O.S." was accompanied by a burst of stars from the Imperial British Infantry, the signal working its way down right into the Canadian lines, where the ammunition was rapidly becoming exhausted.

On account of the trees partially obscuring the flash of the guns of the Imperial battery, the airship that the battery in the château saw did not convey the exact information to the German batteries, and

S.O.S. Stand to!

when they opened up on the château, chunks out of the building and trees and a general ripping up ensued, but their fire did not reach the battery. In all my experience at the front, in three years, I have never known at one time in one spot such a devastating fire as they put over at that particular time. There were over seven batteries—forty guns—ranging from 3 inch to 8 inch, constantly trip-hammering on the building, and the earth trembled and quivered as though in the throes of an earthquake.

Another gun of our Canadian battery of four guns was here put out of action, leaving two guns out of the six. From off my gun we had removed the fallen tree, enabling us to get it into action again. At this time we were receiving the fire from the German batteries on the left rear, left, front and right, leaving only our right rear free from the destruction which was being waged on every other outlet.

Then we gathered up every shell on which we could lay hands,— shells that had been discarded as defective, and rammed them in the guns as fast as our arms and hands would work. At that moment the German airplane returned, flying low and turning his machine gun upon us. We sniped at him with our rifles, but failed to get him.

The Germans had been trying all day to reach Maple Copse, but we held there. Our artillery observer at Zillebeke now phoned that the Huns were massing in Sanctuary Woods—"Fire must come from somewhere." We pulled the last two guns of the Imperial battery and shoved them out in the open; the crews of the remaining guns of this battery were gone; these guns were 4.05's. On they came, and we let them have it beautifully for a good five minutes, and they faltered and fell back. In another ten minutes they came again, when suddenly hell broke loose from our lines,—the Empire batteries had opened up on them. These batteries derived their name from the fact that they were comprised of Australian guns, South African guns, guns from New Zealand, Canada, Scotland, England, in fact every part of the Empire was represented. For a time they smothered the German batteries in Sanctuary Woods. Then a flock of German airplanes flew over these guns and smothered them partially for a few minutes with their machine guns. This entire action had lasted an hour, and at this moment the little relief party, accompanied by our parson, arrived from the wagon lines. Again we were out of ammunition, and the O.C. asked me if I would volunteer to go to the wagon lines after it. "Yes, sir,"—and I mounted the parson's horse and started.

Although it had now started raining, I left the dugout with nothing on but pants, shirt and boots; I had no gas helmet, no coat, no cap, no puttees,—there was no time to be lost—and I was covered with grease and dirt, and must easily have looked like an African.

I had scarcely started when a shell lifted a tree out of its roots and threw it on the road right in front of me, but the horse cleared it with a jump. I passed a dressing station and the sight was unspeakably sad; laid in rows as thickly as they could be placed, the wounded men in all stages of agony were patiently waiting their turn,—ah, God! how patient those men were,—and scattered here and there on both sides of the road were groups of men who had just begun their last sleep, and at sight of them the horse would shy and balk every few yards. I had no spurs with which to control the animal, and my work was cut out for me! he was an ideal parson's horse, for the brute would hardly go faster than a walk. Getting through the gas barrage, I came to a camouflage hedge, used to screen and protect the traffic on the road, which sheltered me for four or five hundred yards further, and then I emerged again into the open, and again I was spotted. At this point a set of new dressing stations had been established, and they were as busy as bees looking after wounded men, and every moment of the time they were engaged in their work the machine guns of the enemy planes were hammering the stretcher bearers and the wounded men as industriously as though they were attacking fighting men. It was quite evident they knew I was a dispatch rider, and I was a target every step of the way, shells being planted before me, behind me and on each side of me. But I knew the Major's thought was with me every foot of the way; I knew he was counting the seconds until I would reach the wagon lines and deliver the message—and the only message—that would save the position; I knew he was praying for me that very moment and I knew that every man in the battery was doing the same thing. If I failed! It was not with me a question of my life; I didn't care a damn for that, and every man of us, on that day anyway, felt the same. But I must

S.O.S. Stand to!

hasten with all the speed that was in me, and I must keep my life, and my head as well, that the others might live.

Finally, I got the horse started on a straight run, came to a bridge crossing the Rampart Canal, but they were shelling the bridge so violently it would have been certain destruction to have attempted getting across. Jumping off, I pulled the horse into a ruined building, and there in the twilight I had a splendid opportunity to view the efficiency of the German observation work. They were making the most determined effort to prevent any communication being sent to the wagon lines for ammunition, and one continual stream of shells was following me down the road; they were dropping as thickly as hailstones for the entire distance up and down the road as far as I could see. I waited there ten minutes and then led the horse out, walking a hundred yards towards the bridge. Then came another burst of shells; again I stopped for a few minutes, made another hundred yards, and another bursting storm of shells. I was walking the horse all this time, but I made up my mind the time had come to make a dash for it. I jumped on his back, lay flat as a pancake, and with a good stout stick I lammed that poor brute as few horses ever were lammed, made a dash for the bridge and got safely across.

About 100 yards over and down came a burst of concussion shells, flying and blowing everything around to smithereens. I was now very close to the square and could see it was being strafed for fair. My experience in watching and timing shell fire now stood me in good stead. I was able by the action of the shells to instantly determine whether the German guns were jumping, rendering their aim uncertain, and, also, to know when the next burst would come, where it would strike, and about how it would operate,—whether gas, shrapnel, or what not. Men were clinging to the walls, trying to take shelter, and it was clearly impossible to get through with the horse. I retraced my steps half way to the ruined building I had just left ten minutes before; I was looking longingly at it, wishing for its friendly shelter, when a shell struck it, blowing it to dust. I then led the horse, hugging the walls as closely as I could, until I got to the edge of the square, then made a run for it across, and had just cleared it when another cluster burst, wounding the horse in the leg. Notwithstanding his wound, he managed to bear me up until I got to

S.O.S. Stand to!

the railroad crossing, lying southwesterly from the square about 500 yards distant. Here the airplane spotted me again and directed a barrage to stop me crossing, but I took the chance and got through it. Every step of the way to the bridge crossing the Yser Canal, shells were being planted at my heels. I can only liken my state of mind to that of the tenderfoot in the saloon of the Wild and Woolly, when Halfbreed Harvey, just for the fun of it, took a revolver in each hand and commenced sending the nuggets of lead into the floor at the unoffending feet of the "Lady from the East," just to see him dance. When I came to within 50 yards of it I saw it was clearly impossible to cross on account of the heavy shell clusters that were raining down.

I waited for a lull in the storm, then slipped on the animal's back, dug my heels in its ribs and rushed for it. I was spattered with mud from head to foot from the exploding shells, but not a single splinter reached me.

As I left the bridge of the canal a hole was blown into it, and a working party, that was kept there all the time for the especial purpose of keeping it in repair, crawled out of their hiding places to engage in their perilous task. It was vitally necessary to keep this bridge intact to facilitate the supplies crossing and recrossing every minute of the night.

The friendly cover of a hedge sheltered me for another hundred yards, and here followed a row of buildings that I hugged until I came to a narrow-gauge trench railroad. Clinging to the walls around were hundreds of wounded men waiting for a conveyance. There was an open stretch from this point and the fliers found me again; their machine-gun fire was directed at once fairly into the middle of the road before me and behind me; their range message was again flashed to their heavies and cobblestones were uprooted and flying everywhere; but the good Lord was with me and I pulled through it. A couple of large trees that had been blown down across the road next intervened, but the horse, lame as he was, cleared them.

I reached the Belgian Château; strafing was going on fearfully in an endeavor to smash the headquarters; men were running hither and thither, stringing telephone wires as quickly as they were shot away; battalions of infantry, fresh troops who had not yet been up the line, were working their way to their destination; chaos seemed to reign on every hand. And yet, there was order. Leaving the Belgian Château, there was a hedge for two or three hundred yards which afforded me cover until I got to the road; there I saw a group of enemy airplanes gradually lowering until they got down to within a few hundred yards of the railroad; they dropped their bombs on the batteries here, starting monster ammunition fires and killing and wounding the gunners.

Although pandemonium reigned everywhere, the guns never hesitated to go on with their work as steadfastly as though they were digging drains in peace time. The fierceness of the fire caused the horse to balk continually, and I again had to get off its back and lead it. This fire was from guns from practically every quarter of the Empire. It was impossible to make any speed now, even with the horse, as the road was black with holes everywhere, and I started to go around what is known as Snake Road. Shells were dropping everywhere; dead horses were piled one on top of the other; huge lorries were lying in the ditches and men were emptying them of their contents and carrying the ammunition on their backs up to the batteries. Here and there were small hills of empty shell cases; there was also considerable danger from the loaded shells that were scattered about that had been spilled from the ammunition wagon, as a kick from the horse on the fuse would have exploded any one of them.

As the lorries advanced up the Snake Road and delivered their ammunition, they left by another road running straight south; this latter was packed with ambulances waiting to take wounded out, and civilians were running madly here and there endeavoring to get out of the fire zone.

I reached Ouderham, which was at that time out of the range of the fire; estaminets were getting ready to close for the night, the hour of ten having struck. The ammunition drivers were lying around taking things easy and not expecting an ammunition call, but the moment I hove in sight they raced out to the wagon line. Many and eager were

S.O.S. Stand to!

the inquiries fired at me as to what was happening up the line. They knew the parson had gone up and they were burning to know what was doing. I told them as well as I could.

"Stand to!" from the Q.M. and they came running from their tents, not waiting to take even a blanket, throwing in their equipment as fast as they could, trotting their horses over to the ammunition trucks and hitching them up.

"Stand to your horses! Prepare to mount! Mount!" came the three distinct orders roared out by the Quartermaster, with scarcely a second's time between each and its fulfillment. With a gunner in each wagon we started in less than eight minutes from the time the order was given, trotting as hard as horses could trot over the cobblestones.

It was not long before we came in contact with the fire, but luck was with us and we escaped until we got to the ammunition dump, where we loaded up with ammunition as fast as men ever worked; it was a joy forever to see those boys work. We had to load up in chain fashion, as it was impossible for the wagons to get to a dump more than four at a time, and the loading was done by the men passing the shells from hand to hand until each wagon was loaded. Then not a second was lost in starting. The crossroads were reached, but the traffic was so congested we could not pass for a while.

Shells were raining down when we finally started, one of them blowing the body off one of our wagons, leaving the limber, but no further damage beyond the driver, Luther, breaking his leg. A gunner took his place and Luther was laid in the gutter until such time as he could be picked up. We galloped past the Empire battery, got to the Belgian Garden at last, taking cover under a clump of trees until the firing had cooled somewhat, and then we took the chance — it was one in ten — to get by. Starting on a dead gallop, shells commenced to chase us all the way up the road. Keeping as well under cover of the hedge as we could, we crossed the railroad bridge, and as we neared the entrance to Ypres square the fire again cooled down; but on getting into the square 25 shells, exploding one after the other as quickly as so many seconds, followed by thunderclaps of brain-splitting noise, ripped up the paving stones,

S.O.S. Stand to!

flinging them in all directions, and taking chunks out of the eight wagons and wheels. Trotting sharply through the square, we got to Rampart Bridge, which they were showering with shells to prevent our engineers repairing it; it was badly smashed and we had to go a long way around by Ypres Rampart.

Here we left the road and took a chance of getting across the open country, picking our way in the fields among the shell holes, eventually getting in back of the Garden, where we strung our wagons in the rear until the order "Ammunition up!" was given, and out from the dugouts rushed the men to unload the precious cargo. Here the captain and lieutenant were wounded, but they refused to go to hospital, saying their wounds were too slight; and, indeed, I can honestly say that every man that night who was wounded and could manage to hold out, did so; each one seemed to be imbued with the idea that his presence was absolutely necessary for the success of the plan in hand.

"You did not need to come back, Grant," said the Major, upon my return. "I intended you should stay at the wagon lines tonight."

"Thank you, sir, but I'd rather be back."

"That's right, that's how we all feel."

That I was more than pleased at this mark of approval from my O.C. goes without saying.

Chains of men formed from the ammunition wagons into the gun pit, shells were passed from hand to hand to the guns where the men were waiting them, and I thought I saw tears of joy in the eyes of the Tommy as he caressed the first shell handed him. "That's for luck," he cried, as he spat on it. The gunners exploded them as fast as they were given them. The work was proceeding nicely when an airplane, flying low over the Garden, spotted our ammunition wagons; he signaled the place back to his batteries and shells from the guns behind hill 60 opened up on us; it became exceedingly violent; many of the horses and wagons were smashed.

This was the order all night long,—wagons arriving with shells, shells passing from hand to hand to the guns, discharged by the

S.O.S. Stand to!

gunners as fast as they were received, and enemy shells rained at us without let-up. We were at our posts all night long. Before daybreak the storm slackened and we got a breathing spell for a few hours.

Immediately after breakfast, at daybreak, the concert opened up afresh, and for full seven days, June 2, to June 9, no man got a full hour's sleep at a time. When not being shelled by the German batteries, the machine gun bullets were raining around; if neither of these agencies of hell were busy, airplanes were flying, many times so low that they seemed to be even with the tops of the trees and singing us their humming hymn of hate. An idea of the deadly nature of the conflict may be had from the first day's casualties, that covered several thousand of our men.

On the seventh day the German fire was so heavy it was impossible to get ammunition up to the guns, and we pulled the backs out of the gun pit as fast as we could smash them, man-handled the guns out of the Garden down on to a little unused road in the rear of the railroad, three-quarters of a mile southwest of the Garden; here the grass was a foot or two in length, and we covered the guns with it and some brush, dug out some large shell holes for them, then the wagons pulled up there, unloading the ammunition, eight hundred to a thousand rounds apiece, and we got orders to open up as an "S.O.S." came from the trenches.

Fritz was not aware of our new position, for his fire was wild, and in the darkness we were safe from the airplanes, although their humming was distinctly audible as they flew here and there vainly looking for our new spot. We worked the guns until 2 o'clock, cleaned them up and got a couple of hours' badly-needed sleep.

At 4:45 A.M. next day another "S.O.S." came from the trenches, and, as fast as we could do so, we let them have it,—this time in Sanctuary Woods. Fritz replied, but his fire was wild. Again the planes came, in an effort to find us, and we got the "keep-firing" whistle. The planes still hovered over us and, under the urgency of a new demand from our trenches, we again had to open up, and this time the plane found us, and the result was quickly seen by a group of visitors breaking directly over us. To register our battery was the work of but a few minutes. The first blast was too far to the right; the

S.O.S. Stand to!

next fell short, and again the correction was made; with just three corrections they had our number; the fourth shell got its mark. The lighter German batteries then passed the range back to the heavies, 5.09 Howitzer batteries, and inside of a minute we were the object of their earnest attention. Their first shell smashed No. 2 gun and crew, leaving us with two guns. We held up our end for half an hour, each moment expecting to get the dose they gave No. 2.

The efficiency of our work was disclosed during the day by the efforts Fritz made to smother us; his fire became so intense we were ordered to leave the battery and take refuge in the basement of a French schoolhouse near by, and from there we had to watch the destruction of our remaining two guns from the concentrated fire of five German batteries of all calibers poured upon them. Our ammunition was completely destroyed, and they struck No. 2 gun repeatedly, but the two other guns were left intact.

It was now about 11 o'clock A.M. and orders were flashed for more guns and more ammunition; then the fire cooled down. During the day two more new guns were brought up, together with one thousand shells, and everything was ready for the retaking of Sanctuary Woods the following morning. Between three and five o'clock the next A.M. the 13th, 15th and 16th Scotch-Canadian Battalion, some of Canada's finest regiments, along with several others, streamed up the road. Wherever the sweep of the kiltie went, there was going to be something doing.

Daylight. "Stand to the battery! Targets, front-line trenches!" We opened up for thirty minutes; our telephonist reported there was such a smoke from the barrage that they could not see the infantry, but the woods were on fire. The Empire battery, together with heavy naval guns that had been brought up, and armored trains, were all concentrating their trip-hammers on the place. It was now evident that every living thing in the woods must be dead, as nothing could live under the hurricane of fire.

We next attacked the road, stopping the German reserves and ammunition from getting near. Then—"Over!"

The net result of the day's work was—the woods, the German front-line trenches, three thousand prisoners, German dead and wounded piled in heaps; wherever the eye turned, the shell holes, trenches and ditches were packed with wounded, dead and dying Huns.

Our captain asked for volunteer observers, and I offered. We went into the place where once was Maple Copse Woods, but it was no more; here and there was a standing tree, but not a leaf or limb left of it, and the trunks were littered with pieces of steel and iron. Before the battle commenced, this spot was one of the loveliest places in the country round about that one could well imagine. Flowers, shrubbery and the rarest of plants of all kinds were there in abundance. This day it was a scarred ruin; the savagery of destruction was so terrible it is indescribable.

We wound our way amongst the dead and the wounded to the top of Mont Soreul, first stopping to take a peep at our old guns; they were still there, but badly battered up; Fritz evidently thought it was barely possible we might have a chance to use them again. We reached our old telephonist's hut on the hill, looked around for Lieutenant Matthews, but he wasn't there; he had been wounded and taken prisoner.

We established lines of communication at once, to hold the Germans back while we built up our own front. Our men were now coming back from their trip and our batteries put up one of the fiercest barrages I have ever witnessed to protect them on their return.

S.O.S. Stand to!

CHAPTER VIII
A BATH UNDER DIFFICULTIES

Over near Hooge was a large naval gun of high velocity and long range, mounted on an armored train. The particular purpose of this nautical monster was to shoot up objects at short notice, such as a body of moving troops, a battery on the road, a train of ammunition wagons. It was concealed in a tunnel made for its specific use, and when it would discharge its missives of destruction it would first project itself from the tunnel, send the message, and then shoot back inside.

Victorious, But Dead Tired

It was at this time paying particular attention to the Square in Poperinghe,—the little station and the hospital there,—and it had become such a diabolical nuisance that it was determined to resort to heroic measures to "get it." A monster balloon was enlisted in the work and the mission of the floating bag was to direct the correspondence of one of our 9.2 naval guns, which was operating on a short railroad built by the Canadian Pacific Railway. This railroad, I may add, has been doing mostly all the track laying and railroad operating for the Canadian forces in Flanders. It was a matter of amazement for the natives to see how quickly a railroad could be placed and operated, and even the soldiers who were all more or less familiar with the workings of this magnificent system in

S.O.S. Stand to!

Canada, were astonished at the speed with which the new machine, especially built by the Company for army purposes, would throw down the rails, fasten them—presto! a railroad to order.

It was resolved that the first work of the balloon should be devoted to putting this German naval gun out of action. In this section at this time the German balloons were thick in the air, and this gave them good control of the Ypres salient. We dared not attempt the experiment there for a long time, but it was finally determined to launch this one, and it was brought up one evening, with its volunteers, inflated during the night, and launched in the morning. Promptly at 10:00 o'clock, when it was ready for raising, the German planes hummed busily overhead. Despite their activities, the balloon got well up and was doing good observation work on its way over to the naval nuisance; there it reached its objective, making the necessary notations and records. Then—Kr-kr-kr-p! Kr-kr-kr-p! And the shells commenced to scatter around it. Then it was a case of getting the bag down, which was not so easy. These observation balloons are operated from a large armored truck, to which they are fastened, and the truck runs along carrying the air-bag with it, attached with a long cable; it is handled just as a toy balloon would be carried by a boy,—when the boy runs along, the balloon runs with him. Attached to the bottom of the gas bag is a basket, usually holding four observers, with a parachute for each man, and while in the air they have to work as fast as possible, because their stay in the azure is as short as the energies of Fritz can make it. If the wind is up and the sky cloudy, it is one chance in a dozen that they will escape before the planes get them, as the swing of the basket makes it difficult in the extreme for them to notice the danger until it is upon them.

On this morning the first indication that they had that their time was up was the swooping down of a cluster of birds of death on all sides. The weather was foggy, a stiff wind blowing and the basket swinging from side to side. This was the first time an attempt had been made to float a balloon in the Ypres salient, as the danger was too obvious to take the risk. However, as I say, the chance was taken. It so happened that our guns were taking a breathing spell, and we stood on the top of our gun pit eagerly watching the fall of the

S.O.S. Stand to!

balloon and its escape. The road along which the armored truck had run ran at one point quite close to the German lines, and the airplanes were now coming thicker every moment and bombing it from every quarter. Telephone and telegraph wires running from trenches to headquarters and all parts of the lines intervened between the balloon and safety, and there was nothing for them but to cut the wires to let the bag get through. Each minute the danger increased, but the men in the truck scrambled up the poles, nipped the wire with their nippers, and the balloon passed through. This was done repeatedly before it reached its haven. Bets were freely made by every man in my gun crew, with the odds of 5 to 1, that the Huns would get it. Somehow I had an inspiration that she would navigate the storm, and I took up all the offers in my battery against the bag—and lost. Her mission of observation had been accomplished, but when she got through the wires she floated to the wagon line, and the result of her arrival here was disastrous in the extreme, as the German shells followed the bag as assiduously as any bunch of schoolboys snowballing a foe, and hundreds of splendid horses were mangled to a jelly by the explosion amongst them.

When it got to the wagon line the crew on the truck commenced to pull it down as rapidly as they could, but when half-way to the ground a flying shell split the cable in twain as neatly as it could have been done with a razor blade, and the bag floated away with the remaining two men out over the German lines. When the descent had commenced two of the crew had taken to their parachutes and got away safely.

Anti-aircraft guns now opened up on it from our lines in an endeavor to destroy it and prevent it getting into the hands of the enemy, and German airplanes and anti-aircraft guns were also firing at it, so that it was a target for all concerned. This, perhaps, is about the only incident in the entire war to date where both the British and the Germans were equally bent upon the destruction of a common object.

The wind suddenly changed and a steady current of air in the other direction brought it back over our own lines; then the two remaining

S.O.S. Stand to!

men seized the opportunity to leave the floater in their parachutes, dropping to safety. A bevy of our planes then went after it, riddled it with rifle bullets, causing the gas to escape, and it finally sank majestically to the ground.

After the battle, I resumed my place at the gun and the usual day's work. Two days later I was detailed to watch for airplanes and was sitting crouched under a culvert, when the familiar humming struck my ear. I could not at first locate it, and crawled out to have a better look skyward, but still failed to place it. Presently the humming stopped, and I thought it had departed, and seized the chance to go to the cookhouse for a cup of tea. When almost there—Kr-kr-kr-p! Kr-kr-kr-p! a slather of German guns had opened upon ours and the fellows fled pell-mell from the gun pit and made for the culvert, taking shelter underneath. They were there about a minute when a shell landed straight on the culvert, going through eight feet of cement and brick, blowing everything in all directions and killing 15 out of the 16 men who had taken refuge there. Less than sixty seconds had elapsed since I left the spot.

When the battle was at its greatest height a wonderful discovery was made. Complaint had been made about the horses dropping on the road on the way up. Some thought it was cramps, others, colic; the veterinary officers were quite puzzled. One night 18 loads of ammunition, three horses to a load, were on their way to the guns and ten of the horses dropped. The vets then took it for granted there must have been poison in the feed, and an examination disclosed that little steel oats were in the grain. The oats had come from the United States and they had been deposited in the grain there.

The discovery was so important that the O.C. offered a prize of five francs to every man discovering these death-dealing pellets in a bag of oats. The bellies of the horses were secure forevermore, as far as these pills of Kaiser Bill were concerned; those five francs did the trick; every grain of the feed that went down the animals' throats first passed an individual examination through the hands of every money-hungry Tommy in the bunch.

After the third battle of Ypres had cooled down, we were permitted to go to the rear as far as Poperinghe, for the purpose of giving

S.O.S. Stand to!

ourselves a scouring, as we were filthy with dirt and lousy with lice. My particular chum on this journey was the little telephonist, Fox, who had been through every big battle up to that time, including the Sanctuary Woods carnage. We got to the wagon lines, eight miles off, by stealing rides on any passing vehicle upon which we could fasten a tooth or a finger nail,—ammunition wagon lorries, ambulances, supply wagons,—as we were thoroughly tired out.

At the wagon lines we persuaded the Q-M to loan us horses for the balance of the journey, which he cheerfully consented to do. But the horses, unfortunately, were mules, practically ready for the bone-yard; the Quartermaster had put them to one side, as they were useless for any further work, and they were awaiting the arrival of the veterinary officer to receive capital punishment. Every time I dug my spurs in my mount, in a mad endeavor to make it go, the only result was a kick in the air with its hind feet.

There was another transportation service in vogue there,—a large number of donkeys, and each time a donkey passed my charger, it would stop dead and wag its ears much after the fashion of a Hebrew gesticulating with his hands in selling a suit of clothes. This was repeated every time we met one of the little donkeys, and each time I had to get off and back the brute for some distance, until it again took the notion to go forward; it was a case of one step forward and two back before I reached my destination.

The most ridiculously funny instance connected with the meeting of the mule and the donkey was the manner in which each indulged in its muleism and donkeyism; the little donkey would shoot its head straight forward, stick its ears out sidewise, at right angles, and commence its song of greeting, which sounded exactly like a man sawing wood, and the mule would warble its well-known lyric of sweetness,—"Hee-Haw! Hee-Haw! Hee-Haw!" keeping time with the flapping of its long lugs.

When I got to Poperinghe Square the mule and myself were all in; save for the ride on the Parson's charger to the wagon lines, I had not been riding for the space of a month, and my legs were so chafed I was compelled to walk like an aged rheumatic for three or four days; but I had company,—the other fellows were similarly affected.

S.O.S. Stand to!

We made our way to the bath in a rush, as every man wanted to be in first. The bath contained 200 men at a time, and 200 tubs; there was no pool in which to bathe; every man had to do his swimming and slopping and washing in a tub; and the sight of the women and girl attendants was a welcome one, as it had been a couple of months before anything feminine had come within the range of our vision. We had to take our turn in going through the routine of the bath.

When I was next, the woman attendant handed me a shirt; a little further along I got a pair of socks, then drawers. Thus equipped, I entered the bathroom; there were about 100 men in there, splashing each other like mad in their wild joy. In stepping along the water-soaked boards, I happened to slip and fall in the wet, and my dry garments were soaked with the water slopped on the boards, assisted by the splashing showers the men were throwing around.

It so happened that one of the fellows had been particularly well splashed by a chum and he was watching for a chance to get even; he determined to wait until his chum had put on his clothes, so that he could execute his vengeance with all the more fullness of perfection. The avenger stood just inside an alley leading to the dressing room, with a pail of water in hand for his intended victim; the water had been scooped out of a tub that had just been used, and it was as dirty as water could be.

As I came even with the alley opening, thinking I was the victim, he let me have it full in the face. I was blinded for a moment with the greasy, soapy, dirty water, and, when my eyes were sufficiently open, it was impossible for me to learn who it was. However, like all things of that kind, I took it in good part and hastened to undress. I filled my tub with pails of water from the tap and started my bath. Oh, how refreshing it was! I don't think I ever appreciated the luxury of a bath until that moment. When through with my ablution it was necessary, before I could dress, to grease my body with a vermin-killer that is supplied the men. This done, I commenced dressing, and had donned my underwear and pants when,—Kr-kr-kr-p! Kr-kr-kr-p!—and a shell landed right in the middle of the bathroom, and the bunch of merry-hearted fellows was transformed into a panic-stricken crowd, leaping and jumping out of the tubs in every

S.O.S. Stand to!

direction in a pell-mell rush, helter-skelter, of men, some half dressed, others absolutely naked, intermingled with the women attendants, in the scramble for safety. Civilians, coming from their houses in a mad rush, added to the confusion.

When the smoke of the explosion cleared, thirty of the bathers lay dead in, on and around the tubs, and forty were wounded, all more or less badly. Inside of three minutes, more shells were planted, some of them landing plumb in the square, and, to my intense sorrow, I learned later that Fox, my little chum, there had paid the supreme price. These shells were totally unexpected, coming from the Hooge district, 11 miles distant.

Everybody sought shelter in the cellars, or any other hole they could crawl into, until night. I searched out my mule, and was thankful to find it where I had left it, tied to a tree, gave it a feed of oats, waited until it munched, unperturbed by the crashing explosions breaking in the immediate neighborhood, and utterly oblivious of the fact that I was counting the seconds until it had finished.

Under cover of the night, I returned to the wagon lines, and in much better time than coming down, for which I had to thank the feed of oats. The bath gave me a new hold on life; I felt ten years younger and several pounds lighter.

I learned next day that the station master at Poperinghe had been arrested, tried as a spy and shot. It transpired that he had a wire running from the station depot straight to the German lines, together with some other signaling apparatus, and there was no doubt in the minds of the trial board that it was due to this man's espionage that the bathers lost their lives while in the tubs.

The spy system had so thoroughly impregnated every hole and corner of the district around Ypres that it became the sorest thorn in the sides of the Command, but we finally managed to root it out hip and thigh, and that sector is now as immune from their activities as any other sector in the front lines.

Going up to take my position with the gun next day I met a bomber of the 21st Canadian Infantry, carrying a bag of his wares—hand

S.O.S. Stand to!

grenades. We walked together for some distance, and just as I was on the point of leaving him to turn off over to my battery I was appalled by one of the most horrifying sights I have seen at the front. One of the pins of a grenade worked loose in the bag and exploded, blowing his right hand and leg completely off. I have seen scores of happenings, each of which in its entirety was a thousand times more terrible, but there was something about the suddenness, the total unexpectedness, and the fearful spurting of his life's blood, that filled me more full of horror than anything before or since.

In this conflagration that is shaking the world, death stalks on every hand in a hundred different forms, entirely apart from the destruction that the enemy can bestow. I was standing but three feet behind him. As quick as I could I gave him first aid and yelled for a stretcher, but there was nothing that could be done; he lived until sundown.

S.O.S. Stand to!

CHAPTER IX
HAMBONE DAVIS

One evening we were sitting outside of our bivouac watching some German balloons being downed by one of our airplanes; our flier had good luck that evening, accounting for three of the floating sausages; and as we were awaiting the finish of the last sausage, and speculating on how long it would take our air bird to get it, or whether he would get it at all, the gambling spirit ran rife, and fast and furiously the bets were placed.

Open-mouthed and eager we watched and, while watching, a strange-looking figure of a soldier ambled, or shuffled, up the path toward our place. He was a man about 45, though looking more like 55, quite grizzled, furrowed face, and a stubby mustache, thickly stained with tobacco juice, decorated his upper lip. He was chewing tobacco as if his life depended on the quantity of juice he could extract from each mouthful, and dried tricklings of the liquid ornamented his chin. As he came toward us his face was turned upward, taking in the scrimmage in the sky. "What's them bloody things?" he asked, indicating the air sausages. He had evidently just come up the line fresh from England. I told him and he jerked out an indelible pencil and made a note, sucking the lead of the pencil two or three times before he finished, and this habit, continuous with him, kept his lip constantly stained with the indelible lead.

Just then a mighty roar of delight went up from the entire crowd, as our bird gobbled the last remaining sausage, but our indelible friend paid no attention to the uproar,—he simply took out his little book and made another note.

The "Fall-in!" whistle was blown and we were a bit surprised as well as amazed to see our strange friend fall in in front, still chewing vigorously; he evidently didn't know or didn't care a damn whether it was against the rules to chew tobacco when parading. The Sergeant-Major eyed him curiously and then stepping to his side whispered something; we knew he was explaining to him that he was infringing orders, but a non-commissioned officer is not permitted to bawl out another non-com in the presence of the men. Hastily bestowing the quid in his hand he stood to attention. Roll call finished and we retired to our bunks.

Early next morning when we emerged from our quarters the first person we saw was the odd-appearing individual that had joined up with us the night before, with his inevitable note book in his hand. He was still busily sucking his indelible pencil in the corner of his mouth, and, in the light of the morning sun, there was nothing about his mug that was any more prepossessing than appeared in the twilight of the previous night. He also had on the sleeve of his coat a crown, indicating that he was to be our acting Sergeant-Major in the absence of the regular officer, and when not so acting, he was to be the First Sergeant of the section.

The official activity of our new friend commenced to be evidenced in a number of ways; he lost no time in making us understand that he was First Sergeant. "Sergeant Grant, detail two men for the cookhouse!" Then to the gunners, "Here, you, clean up your wagons and take off all that mud; it's filthy"; this was absolutely unnecessary and the fellows swore vehemently under their breath; to the drivers,—"Clean up that 'ere 'arness and get that mud hoff it"; he also compelled us to burnish the steel and made the gunners scrub the paint off the brass and sandpaper it up. This necessitated the men going to a shop and purchasing the sandpaper themselves, as disobedience of the order meant a sojourn in the clink and the excuse that he had no sandpaper would not go.

By the time old Sol had reached the meridian, the First Sergeant had succeeded in getting himself thoroughly hated, and many and earnest and unique were the resolutions to "get even." This feeling was intensified by his order to gather up some scantlings of hard wood and bring them to his quarters; he was a sort of a one-horse carpenter by trade and had started manufacturing for his own especial use and benefit a wooden structure large enough to house himself.

The idiosyncrasies of our newfound friend manifested themselves variously, the first and chief characteristic by which he came to acquire the *sobriquet* of "Hambone Davis," was his habit of heading

S.O.S. Stand to!

for the cookhouse each morning before the men were dismissed from the horse lines—which was necessary before we could appease our always ravenous appetites—so that he could garner for himself an edible that was longed for and looked for by every man who could get it, i.e., the ham bone, because there were always more or less pickings on it and he was a lucky fellow indeed who was successful in capturing the prize. But, in his official capacity, Davis was able to get out and get over there ahead of us every morning and during his entire stay in our crowd, he was the only man who each morning got the ham bone. Hence his cognomen.

Long, earnest and secret conferences were had as to the way we had best settle our grievances. Among the conspirators were Dynamite Pete, so-called because of his habit of taking shells, fuses and bombs apart and examining and prying into their contents. One time his curiosity came nearly getting him a quick passage West. He was examining a bomb and, taking out the pin, was holding it in his hand, looking at it for a brief instant. Providentially an officer was standing beside him who saw his mad act and, grabbing the bomb from his hand, flung it into the field—and just in time! It exploded before it had well gotten on its way.

Pete's answers to the officer, while respectful, were tantalizing to a degree:

"What did you do that for?"

"What are they here for?"

"Why did you take the pin out?"

"Because it is made to come out."

"Did you want to kill yourself?"

"If I did it would have been my own funeral."

"How about the others?"

"They had no business here."

"Think it over in the clink—ten days."

S.O.S. Stand to!

I could think of nothing else but the fellow who was passing a private residence one day with a pitchfork on his shoulder, and a big dog came rushing out at him, and he jammed the dog through with his pitchfork, killing him. The owner came out in a great rage.

"What did you do that for?"

"What did your dog run at me for?"

"Why didn't you hit him with the other end?"

"Why didn't he come at me with his other end?"

Gunboat Stevens was another of the plotters; his suggestions were so unique and uncommon that each of them sent us into an uncontrollable roar of laughter. Unfortunately, as we thought, they were usually as impracticable as they were strange. This member of our gang derived his alias from his warm adherence to the navy as against the army. Never was there an argument started about the navy that it did not have a burning advocate in Stevens; he would even go to the length of challenging any man in the crowd to fight him then and there who had the temerity to claim that the Empire had as good a defender in the military as in the naval arm of the government.

We also had a Jesse James; his surname was really James and it was easy fitting on the handle.

The conference finally resolved itself into a determination to burn his new-made bivouac, but I dissuaded them and convinced them that it would be much better for them to lug it over to the incinerator and throw it into the pit. To complete the plot and give it an artistic finish, it was necessary to have a ham bone, and Gunboat volunteered to get it. "I'm on picket tonight," he said, "and I'll go to the cookhouse when the cook is asleep and fix it." He did so; when the cook was dreaming of everything but the front line, Gunboat quietly slipped in, unearthed the ham that was in readiness for our breakfast, and with his knife he quickly extracted the bone, taking care of the pickings with his teeth while finishing his sentry go.

S.O.S. Stand to!

The next night everything was in readiness and when the opportune moment arrived, with Hambone leaving with ammunition for the guns, I passed the word. When he was well on his way we hurried over to his shack, rooted it out and carried it bodily over to the incinerator, setting it completely over the hole. Now for the artistic touch. We took the ham bone, fastened it with wire to the end of a stick that we nailed across the top of the shack, with the end protruding well out to the side, and on the end of the ham bone we hung a placard, so that all could see, reading, "Here lies the remains of Hambone Davis. Gone but not forgotten." Then we scampered over to one side and with the glee of mischievous schoolboys watched developments. Nearly every passing soldier, noticing the odd sight, strolled over and read the sign, going off snickering.

The following evening Hambone arrived back from the guns; he had with him some of the conspirators carrying wood that he wanted; it was the first time they experienced real pleasure in that work because they foresaw the dénouement in store.

When they reached the spot where his home had been, Hambone looked around in a dazed sort of fashion, almost swallowing a mouthful of tobacco juice as he blurted out, "Where the bloody 'ell is my 'ouse? What bloody well nonsense is this? Hi'll make someone pay for this!" The rest of us were loitering in the immediate vicinity, listening with sheer chucklings to his burning vows, and it was all we could do to stifle our laughter. Then Hambone ran around like a looney, looking here and there for his house, and when he found it and saw the bone and read the placard, his feelings were so intense that he actually spat out his mouthful of tobacco, juice and all.

"'Ere, you lobsters! You, Grant, who has done this?"

"I don't know; how should I know?"

"Hi bet you do know!"

"Aw, what the hell are you getting at? Don't try any of that on me or I'll have you up for office," I threatened.

He didn't seem to be getting anywhere in his efforts to find out the guilty ones, so he did the next best thing.

S.O.S. Stand to!

"Sergeant Grant, take six of your men and put that 'ouse back." There was nothing for it but to obey, but I made a mental resolve he would never sleep in that shack that night at least. We took hold all together and lifted it up, and on the way over I purposely stumbled in such a way that the mansion of Hambone fell on one corner and with the fall it came tumbling to pieces.

Our arch-enemy composed himself to sleep that night in the guard room, as none of us would give him room in our quarters, and it so happened that Gunboat Stevens was in the clink at the time for having called him "Hambone." They occupied the same room, his bed immediately opposite the First Sergeant's, with just a foot or two of space between the bottom of each bed. As may be imagined, no kindly good nights passed between the two.

Now Davis had just been over from England but a short time and was comparatively clean in his person, while Stevens was lousy, and to complete the diabolism of the revenge, Gunboat, instead of throwing his shirt on the floor as he usually did, watched his opportunity and when he heard a snore from Hambone that had no camouflage in it, he slipped his shirt in at the head of the bed where our official tormentor reposed.

Our glee was positively fiendish next day when watching Hambone wriggling uneasily in his clothes at parade. Gunboat had sent us an underground message telling us what he did, and we did not fail to recognize the symptoms at once; every moment he got a chance he was scratching himself; and as soon as he had the opportunity he made for the nearest tree and, rubbing his back violently against it, almost wore a hole in his coat. Miserable were his moments throughout that day. "'Ow in 'ell can a man fight an' scratch at the same time!" he would snort.

There was no let up to his officiousness, however; his damnable orders were as numerous as before; so we concluded to hatch a scheme that would most effectively put him on the blink, and the opportunity occurred the very next night. Hambone was detailed to proceed to the guns, to relieve the Sergeant-Major there, and it was his duty to take charge of the supply wagon that carried the supplies for the men there, and by chance there was among the rations this

S.O.S. Stand to!

time a jar of rum. Accompanying Hambone were Snow and Reynolds of our section, they sitting in the back end of the wagon. They had barely started when Snow discovered the rum jar, and he and Reynolds at once got their wits working as to how they could get away with it. When about half-way there, Hambone, to stretch his legs, got off the wagon and walked alongside, and Snow instantly whispered to Reynolds, "get off and walk with him and tell him you hear a shell coming." Reynolds did as directed and Hambone ducked for cover and the wagon stood stock still. No sooner was the First Sergeant's back turned than Reynolds threw the jar into the ditch.

A minute or two elapsed and no explosion taking place, Hambone rejoined the wagon and the party proceeded. Then Snow slipped off the back and went back for the jar, but instead of going up the road, he took the railroad track, beating the wagon by some minutes and hiding his jar of joy in my gun pit, immediately got back and was standing beside the wagon when it arrived. Hambone seeing him there hadn't the remotest idea that he had hopped off at any time, and supposed that he had ridden the entire way with them. Snow gave Reynolds the wink and he knew the prize was safe.

The first thing Hambone did was to go to the back of the wagon for the jar. It was gone! He searched wildly about for a moment, asking first one and then the other what had become of it, and Snow volunteered the opinion that probably it had dropped off when the wagon lurched that time he thought the shell was coming. There was nothing for it but to report his loss, and the only excuse he could give was that the rum had probably rolled off when they trotted at a coming shell, and what the officer didn't say to Hambone for trotting, which was a violation of orders, would not be worth repeating. He bellowed at him to go and search for it, and with wicked delight we watched the duffer going back over the route, peering from side to side of the road in his vain search.

The journey was a nine-mile trot and he covered more than half the distance, endeavoring to find the precious container, and when he came back in a couple of hours without it, the poor devil thought he was going to be licked, such was the anger of the men at missing

S.O.S. Stand to!

their rum rations, because they sorely needed it; none but those who have been there can and do appreciate how sorely it is needed in that region of the world.

I make no apology or attempt to excuse myself as an accessory after the fact. It is an unwritten law among the men that the only crime involved in stealing liquor is—using an Irishism—not to steal it.

The only men in the section that night who had a ration of the treasured fluid were Dick Snow, Reynolds and myself, and in the midst of our conviviality we prophesied that if Hambone survived this disaster, he was immortal.

Toasting the health of the King, the army, the navy and our loved ones at home, we retired in blissful consciousness of a good job well done.

Next morning, black looks and cursing threats in low voices greeted Hambone on all sides, and his work that day was so fidgety, and he made so many mistakes in getting the ranges on the sights, that the Major performed the *coup d'état* for which we were all anxiously waiting by transmitting as quickly as he could to headquarters his recommendation that he be retired, and Hambone, to our immense relief, was shipped back to England.

S.O.S. Stand to!

CHAPTER X
BEES, HONEY AND HELL

On Tuesday, August 29, 1916, my battery pulled into Martinsaart, in the Somme district, which lies three miles immediately west of Thiepval. The Battle of the Somme had been raging since July 1. We took up our position in a beautiful orchard, its trees laden down with apples, and along the hedge on one side of the orchard were ten beehives, humming and throbbing with busy bee life. Underneath some large apple trees we placed our guns and the thickly woven hedge right in front of us gave us a splendidly concealed nook; through the hedge we cut a hole for our beauty's nozzle.

At 5:15 in the afternoon we started registering our "love letters," in preparation for another phase of the big bombardment which had been more or less continuously in operation since the commencement of the battle, and after accomplishing our purpose we got a "stand down." The apples clustering on the trees looked as tempting to us as did the apple of our first father and before we started registering, every man in the battery had mentally made his tree selection as the one he would climb as soon as he got a minute to himself. It was unnecessary to climb, however; with the advent of the explosion of our guns, the concussion shook the trees as with a strong wind and the luscious fruit showered upon our heads in abundance.

Then we cleaned up our guns, munching the red apples, and the enemy planes were humming like bees over our heads, darting here and there like bats, trying to find our place of concealment, but we were too well hidden. When night fell, McLean and I started for the rear, passing the hives on our way. "By, Golly, Grant, here's a chance for a mouthful; I know how to handle this proposition," and he made for the hives. He lifted off the top, with the bees flying all around, and handed me the top to hold while he inserted his hand and took out a comb, which he passed over to me, saying, "Take this till I get another, the damned bees are stinging me." Thousands were around him. I took it and started on the dead run for my billet, about 400 yards away, and in a minute or two Mac followed with another

S.O.S. Stand to!

comb. The fellows greeted us with exclamations of delight and surprise; many of us had been two years in the battle line without ever having seen, let alone tasted, such a delicious morsel. Every man in the billet fell to, munching the honey with expressions of sheer joy; every fellow in the bunch had his face and hands littered with the sticky joy like so many kids munching taffy. In the midst of our feasting, visitors called; the robbed bees came flying into the room after their treasure. McLean, by this time, had been stung about twenty times, and I had about a dozen nips on my hands and face, and in the very heat of our argument with our visitors, "Stand to!" was sounded, and honey, bees and everything else was dropped as we raced for the guns. But the bees did not drop us; they chased us every bit of the way; they attacked our hands, our mouths, our necks,—wherever there was a particle of our anatomy exposed we were stung.

On our way to the guns McLean brought a comb with him, leaving the other alongside his bed. We had to pass the Major on our way, whose dugout was close to the hives, and by that time he had an inkling of what was going on and he yelled, "Grant, throw that honey down; you too, McLean." As he yelled his orders I was passing the telephonist's hut and I threw it in to him,—"Here, Graham, here's some honey for you, it's great," and continued my run down to the guns, the bees still following us up.

McLean laid his comb on a pile of shells beside the gun, and the heat of the August day caused the honey to trickle over the shells. I commenced pointing the gun while Mac worked the range drum; the angles were passed to us and inside of a minute we were firing, and inside of another minute we had the sternest kind of a battle on our hands, for thicker than ever the bees came swarming around the gun.

"Who in hell broke into those hives?" yelled the Major.

No reply; we were busily working and "hadn't time" to answer. The honey on our hands, coupled with the dust, made a grit that in opening and closing the breech caused the mechanism to stick, and the honey clinging to the shells caused the breech chamber to stick, making the shell cases jam in the gun after being discharged, forcing

S.O.S. Stand to!

us to pry open with a sharp pick the breech each time to extract the empty cartridge. All during the operation the Major was cursing like a madman at the men, whoever they were, that brought the bees into the business.

It was my duty to set the sight, and as I did so, each time, the bees would attack my hands and head, and in trying to attend to the sight and wipe the bees off at the same time, my work was harder than can well be imagined; but poor Billy's case was even harder, he had to keep a steady hold of his range drum with both hands and he couldn't budge to brush off his attackers, as it was absolutely necessary to hold dead steady to enable us to do our shooting accurately.

"Grant, for God's sake knock this bee off my neck," he pleaded; "it's stinging hell out of me"; but every time I made a move to help him, the Major roared, "Get that angle on, Grant; get your range on, McLean." And we had to take our medicine. Parker, who was passing shells, was in the same plight as the rest of us; his hands were covered with the sugary fluid that had settled between the copper splinters of the driving bands on the shells and the slivers were slitting his hands. This is a necessary accompaniment that the men passing the shells into the gun have to contend with, and ordinarily it is a sore and painful piece of business, but in conjunction with the swarm of the bees it was simply hellish.

A change of angle was momentarily expected from the observer; we had been looking for it for some minutes, and the Major was beginning to rave and rant, very much like a theater manager when the star has not yet put in her appearance and the impatient audience on the outside are giving vent to catcalls. He could stand it no longer and ran as fast as his legs would carry him over to the telephonist's hut; there he found Graham crouching alongside of his telephone in the folds of a blanket over his head and face. It was the usual field telephone that we used, in conjunction with a telegraph buzzer, and Graham was endeavoring to deliver his messages and fight off the bees at the same time, while bringing to his aid the smoke of a fag that he was endeavoring to puff into the faces of his antagonists in the hope that it would help some.

S.O.S. Stand to!

The Major bellowed, "You damned jackass! take off that blanket. What do you mean?" Graham threw off the blanket and started working his buzzer, but the bees had as little regard for the rank of the Major as they did for that of Sergeant Graham, and three or four of them kept pinging away at him, but as long as the Major was there his splendid discipline enabled him to do his work. He got into communication at once with the trenches, gave us our new targets and we kept on with our work until darkness prevented further registering that night, although the twilight still prevailed.

"Stand down!" came the order. "Clean up guns and lay on S.O.S. lines for the night," meaning to load the gun with a fuse shell timed for a certain range, or to burst on percussion, just as the target requires, safety catch down, sight set, range on range drum and the gun laid on a predetermined point to be covered, in both cases being the front line trench, although it might be a machine-gun emplacement, barbed-wire, bombing post, crossroads or observation station. For a front-line trench and an attack started by the enemy, the S.O.S. signal is passed from the trench, either through the telephonist in the trenches, or by means of colored star shells. Immediately upon receipt of this signal by our S.O.S. sentry or the telephonist at the battery, we get the order "S.O.S. stand to the battery," and in the space of four seconds from the time we receive that order, our first shell must be exploded in the German lines under pain of the severest penalty. If a man were taking a wash, he would have to jump out of the water and get to the guns as quickly as God and nature would permit him.

Before retiring for our billets, Mac and I decided that we might as well get some more honey, as we felt that the bees had done about all that they could to us and we were deserving of a little further reward for what we had endured, and arming ourselves with smoke helmets, we made a further sortie on the camp of our winged enemies. As fast as if I were ramming home a shell, I lifted off the hive while Mac pulled out a couple of combs swarming with bees. We thought we were making a good job of it this time and getting away scot free, when suddenly I felt a stab under my coat sleeve and almost at the same moment Mac had the same experience and we broke into a run for the billet. By the time we got there we were

S.O.S. Stand to!

being stung frightfully on our bodies, as the bees had made their way up under our shirt sleeves and we ripped off our coats and shirts, fighting the common enemy at the same time. The boys in the billet beat it outside while we "carried on."

After a vigorous battle we seemed to have the foe beaten into submission and the fellows returned; then we had a feed of honey, hung up the remainder on the wall and retired for the night. Mac retired to his bunk first and had scarcely settled down when he emitted another snort, then a yell; the bees had settled in between the blankets of his bed and were renewing their onslaught on his helpless body.

Everybody started laughing at McLean's plight, but no sooner were the rest of us settled down till we too had a battle on our hands; and in the middle of the fray, Fritz started shelling our billets with gas shells, one of the missiles going clean through the tile roof and knocking the tiles down on our heads. Then came a salvo—six shells—followed by several others. "S.O.S." was signaled and "Stand to," and out we raced for the guns, sans shirt, sans everything, bumping into the trees on our way and falling in shell holes in the orchard.

The gas they were putting over at this time was more dangerous than any I had yet experienced, it having a more direct effect on the lungs than any they had yet given us. It had started to rain and the darkness was black, but we reached the guns within scheduled time, and under great difficulty we exploded our shells; but most of our work in that discharge was guesswork.

It soon cooled down and we again sought our billets after laying the guns on "S.O.S." and even the pain from the stings of the bees did not prevent us getting into dreamland in short order.

At 3:30 in the morning I went out to visit the last guard shift, as was my duty. Then, dawn breaking over the land, I went out to see what damage the shells had done, and on the way I stumbled into a crop of the most delicious mushrooms. Off came my helmet and I filled it to the brim and hastened to the cookhouse with them; he had just got his fire started and I asked him if he would oblige me by cooking them for me, as I wanted them for my gun crew, and he gladly complied with my request.

Then cookhouse was called and the crew came to breakfast and when each man got his portion of the mushrooms served him, his astonishment was as great as when he got the honey. So that between the honey and the dewy dainties I had gathered, together with a couple of jars of pickled pork and two small jars of rolled butter found in one of the vacated cellars by an industrious member of our crew, you can imagine the excited condition of our minds that morning at breakfast.

During the course of the feasting the Sergeant-Major arrived on the scene. "Well, for Heaven's sake! Who was the guy that got the mushrooms?" He was informed that I was the lucky individual and he asked me if I would show him the way, and I was just directing him when "Stand to the battery!" intervened, and we bolted for the guns and opened up. "Fifty rounds gunfire" was ordered; then "Second fire ten seconds," then "Second fire five seconds," then "Gunfire steady"; next, "Independent fire ten seconds"; then came the order for a sweeping fire to enable our infantry to dig in in a trench they had just taken, and to prevent Fritz getting it back. Our work was accomplished and "Stand down and lay on day lines!" was ordered and I was cleaning the sight of my gun and wiping off the effects of the gas fumes when the Sergeant-Major came along and asked me to indicate where I had gathered the mushrooms; I pointed the spot out to him, and he made a bee line. In a couple of minutes I heard him calling and I looked up, "Here's a beauty you missed, Grant; you must have been blind," and he held up a mushroom as large as a breakfast plate. I laughed and replied, "Yes, you are lucky, Sergeant-Major." Then Kr-kr-kr-p! Kr-kr-kr-p! and Fritz started getting busy again as an airplane hovered about, and the pace getting too deucedly hot, we started for the trenches; it was a ditch-trench half full of water which came to our waists, and in it we paddled our way until we got to a fairly good trench, and on the journey down imprecations of all kinds were hurled on the head of the offending Sergeant-Major. "Where is that damned fool of a Sergeant-Major?" asked one; "It was his gathering those mushrooms in the open that started Fritz." Just at that moment down the ditch

S.O.S. Stand to!

came the Sergeant-Major limping; he had been slightly wounded in the leg by a bit of shrapnel, but he was hanging onto his mushrooms.

"'Ere, Grant, take this, will you, till I fix me leg," and he handed me the mushrooms and started undoing his puttee where the blood was soaking through. When he had bound up his wound I handed him his dainties and he held them up admiringly.

"It was a bit dangerous, doncher know, but, blow me tight, if I wouldn't do it again to get a beauty like that," holding up the large one he had shown me when he was gathering them.

"You bleedin' idiot," I said, "don't you know a mushroom when you see it? That's a toadstool! I passed it up."

S.O.S. Stand to!

CHAPTER XI
SCOTTY COMES BACK AT THE SOMME

The German lines were on the hills; every time we took a position it was always uphill, until we got over Pozières Ridge and then our work was downhill for the time. We arrived at the firing line on the 29th of August, 1916. The accompanying map will convey a general idea of the object intended to be attained by the great drive. The German organization in this district was fed by railroads having terminals at Bapaume and it was clearly evident that with this city in our possession the supply organization of the enemy would be largely demoralized. Hence the plan. Bapaume lay southwest from our trenches a matter of 15 miles; intervening were the towns of Labazell, Pozières, Courcelette and Martinpuieh,—all on the Albert-Bapaume road.

We arrived just in time to save Pozières. The Australian boys had driven their way clean through to this place, but had not sufficient reënforcements to hold it, and were being exterminated when we reached the point and saved them with our guns and the wonderful work of our infantry in driving the Boches half-a-mile over the ridge. The opportunity for Canada to assist her sister dominion was a matter of profound thankfulness to every man of us; to lend a helping hand under such circumstances was indeed cheery work.

The Imperial troops and Australians, under great difficulties, had blasted their way into Labazell, the crater of the mine blown up being one of the largest I have seen on the Western front. This was the commencement of the Somme offensive and happened on the 1st of July, 1916. When I reached this crater two battalions of Canadian troops were stationed in its depths in holes burrowed all around the sides, and it was used as an assembling point for reënforcements. This will convey an idea of the extent of the mining operations.

The distance from the mine to our new position was three-quarters of a mile and the ground was billeted with corpses all the way to our battery; in the crater itself it was impossible to step without walking on bits of human bodies, and the dugouts surrounding were filled

S.O.S. Stand to!

with German dead; there were thousands of them. It was so manifestly impossible to give them any sort of a burial that the order was issued to fill in the dugouts where they lay and this was done by heaving the ground in on top of them. Never to my dying day can I forget the sight of those German dead! Dead everywhere! In whatever direction the eye turned there were the rigid warriors of the Kaiser cold in death. It was many nights before I could get a straight sleep without seeing mortifying Huns. But I have long since ceased to have any pity for them. Although they are the victims of a system over which they have no apparent control, yet they are supposed to be human beings with human, red blood in their veins, and the numberless deeds of which they have been guilty have branded them as nothing better than brute beasts in the eyes of all humanity.

With the help of the Pozières Ridge we could observe Fritz quite clearly now, and every time he attempted any digging-in work our guns would speak to him in terms so convincing that he fain would desist. My battery then moved up to within a thousand yards of the foe, one and a half miles northwest of Labazell, where we had to dig right in the open. At this point the dead were also strewn so thickly that it was practically impossible to walk without stepping on a corpse, or part of one, every other step, among them being many of our own fellows who here paid the supreme price, and each time we came across a laddie in khaki it was a signal for an outburst of swearing. Had we not sworn we would have wept, and, naturally, as men we preferred to do the other thing.

While here our rations ran short; our prisoners numbered over 20,000 and the policy of the British Government being to treat a prisoner as well, if not better, than her own soldiers (their wants are always attended to first), we were practically without food, and were compelled to resort to the heroic method of taking the rations from the bodies of our poor comrades who were lying cold on the ground and who would need them no more.

Three-quarters of a mile north of Labazell we were in our gun pit one night and "Ammunition up!" was the order. This meant that everybody, including officers and down to cook, the telephonist on

S.O.S. Stand to!

duty alone being excepted, had to get out and help unload the life-saving material. I remember thinking of the anomaly at the time,—how strange it was that we should regard the ammunition as life saving, when it was in reality so destructive of life. While working like Turks unloading the shells, some of the drivers were talking about a strange sight they had seen down the road near Albert (pronounced Albare), when loading up at the ammunition dump. They told us that huge contraptions covered with tarpaulin were lying on the side of the road, with six-pounder guns protruding from their sides; in conversation the drivers referred to them as land boats, and some, as land dreadnaughts. Speculation ran rife as to their purpose. We were soon to see. Next morning as dawn was breaking, "Stand to!" rang out. Waiting in our gun pits for the next command, I heard the sound of an engine put-put-ing along the road, something akin to that of a machine gun, but yet different.

I looked in the direction of the sound and presently there hove in sight a colossal something of behemoth proportions;—something the like of which I had never seen or heard of in all my life, and I was stricken dumb with amazement. A monstrous monstrosity climbed its way without let or hindrance, up, over, along and across every obstacle in its path. Presently it reached the top of Pozières Ridge; every man who could see had his eyes glued on it. It came down the ridge at about five miles an hour with two small guns peering out of each side. It was the first tank! We all thought at first it was an armored car of some kind. Then it swung off the road, crossing a ditch 8 feet wide and 17 deep and when we saw it perform this stunt our faculties were for the moment spellbound, and then we burst into uncontrollable cheering.

From all quarters of the valley soldiers were running to see the absurdly strange sight; it was as if a general fire alarm had been sounded, with everybody hastening to the scene of the conflagration. Passing close by our battery, it paused for a while, and I had the opportunity of giving it the once-over, and then it waddled on its way again. In a few minutes two companion land boats made their début amongst us; up they went over the ridge, rolling down the German barbed-wire entanglement as if it were so much thread and forcing huge gaps for the Infantry to pass through, continuing their

S.O.S. Stand to!

way placidly on through the trenches of the Hun, flattening scores of German soldiers under their bulk who were too awe-stricken to move.

Our Infantry then took up the beaten path, charging the enemy trenches, and Fritz was an easy prey that morning.

Inside of half an hour after our tanks reached the lines of Fritz, the prisoners in gray commenced to stream toward our lines; for a distance of seven miles the road was jammed with captured Huns. Some of them passing by our battery spoke to me in English, as good as, if not better, than my own, and asked me what in hell was the meaning of waging war in such fashion; they referred to the tank as Landfuerchtenichts. I told them that was nothing to what was in store for them. "Why," I said, "I've got reserved seats on one of them for Berlin."

"You'll never get that far," he retorted.

The action on the Somme was well under way when one morning at daybreak, making my way to the cookhouse, I was greeted, "Hello, Grant, hoos awa' wi' ye, laddie? Ma sontes, but you're lookin' fine! An' damned if he isn't a Sergeant!" It was Scotty, reinstated in our unit in his former capacity of cook, and he had brought with him his nerve, his twinkle, his bow legs and all. I must confess I was glad to see him, and when we had a few minutes together he told me, with all the gusto imaginable, of his exploits in London.

With his little eyes twinkling like pin points, he related how England needing every available man, he was reinstated, and having observed strict military discipline while in the camp he was, under the rule, entitled to back pay, so that he had a year's wages coming. He obtained leave of absence, hastened to London and procured in some manner a British Major's uniform, in which he disported himself in first-class hotels, restaurants and the like, receiving the homage that became a returned fighting man, in the shape of dinner engagements, theater invitations and drinks galore. The deception was discovered and he was clinked for thirty days, at the end of which he was packed off to the front lines.

He wound up by telling me that, he expected to get into the game shortly, as he wanted to be in it when the Germans got what was coming to them.

We were occupying at this time some splendid dugouts and trenches that we had taken from Fritz; they were made of chalk as was also the cookhouse. Of our battery of sixteen guns at this point my gun was nearest to the cookhouse, and I was mightily tickled at the prospect of having an opportunity now and again to slip in and have a drink of hot tea, or something of the kind, with my old friend.

Ex-German "Pill Box" That Is Now a British Dugout

That night I dropped in on Scotty and casually remarked that our guns would speak shortly and I expected we would bring the German fire upon us, as was the usual result. Scotty's voice quavered I thought, as he asked me when we would begin. "Oh, in an hour, maybe. Have you got a sup of hot tea, Scotty?" "No, I hae na tea, Grant; you'll get your tea at the proper time and not before." "Well, of all the— —." I couldn't find words, and then I remembered his old-time habit of thriftiness, and I made up my mind to keep a sharp lookout, and if I caught him profiteering in rations he had

S.O.S. Stand to!

saved from the men, I mentally resolved I would show him no mercy.

Exactly at 2 o'clock that morning we started sending our messages to Fritzie, and inside of a minute—Kr-kr-kr-p! Kr-kr-kr-p! Kr-kr-kr-p! Kr-kr-kr-p! And his shells were flying all around us. The cookhouse was only about 20 yards off and I wondered if Scotty would now loosen up a bit, and I stepped over leaving Lawrence in charge of the gun. The cook had crawled under his bunk, which was merely a slight wire mattress raised a couple of feet off the floor. There was a dixie of hot tea standing near and I started to help myself to a drink. He saw what I was doing and with chattering teeth told me he would report me in the morning. He had scarcely spoken when a shell tore through the cookhouse, going clean through the wall over his bed, and as the roar of it passed by, I heard Scotty again offering up supplications in a manner that would arouse the admiration of the most earnest camp-meeting devotee. The shells were commencing to pop all around and I knew instantly that Fritz had located the cookhouse instead of the battery, and I roared to Scotty to come out, but he wouldn't budge. I reached under and grabbed him by the leg, dragging him to the door and leading him by the hand, for he was shaking like a leaf, made my way to the battery. By that time Fritz had got a better line on the guns and it was getting so hot that we got orders to retire to our dugouts. I pushed the cook ahead of me and when we got to the path leading to our quarters, about 200 yards off, no sprinter ever lived that could equal the pace of the bow-legged chef. I doubt if a moving picture machine could have caught the flash of his legs.

The following day we got the welcome order of billets. When there the O.C. made an announcement that he would give a prize of 20 francs to the driver of the best pair of mules on inspection day, which was two weeks hence. This was done for the purpose of encouraging the well-being of the animals,—a most important factor in our own well-being. Scotty's eye to thrift ever open, he entered into an engagement with one of the drivers that he would feed his mules potato peelings if he would split fifty-fifty with him on the prize. The driver agreed and a few days later he and his helper appeared at the door of the cookhouse with one of the mules to get his feed. In order to prevent spilling the peelings at the entrance to the cookhouse, he backed the mule up against the door. In France, as is well known, every farmhouse has a cesspool in which all manner of refuse is distilled by means of a pump and straw, and used to fertilize the soil. These pools are all the way from 8 to 10 feet deep. Immediately in front of the cookhouse and the mule was one of these cesspools, our billets here being on a farm. It happened that when Scotty was peeling his potatoes that day, he had thrown them so close to the fire that they got thoroughly heated. He hastily gathered them up and threw them in a pan which he handed to Tompkins, the man who had charge of the mules and who had entered into the agreement with him; the driver was still on the animal's back. When the mule stuck his nose into the hot peelings he jerked backwards into the door of the cookhouse, the driver's back struck the wall over the entrance and he was shot clean off the mule's back headforemost into the cesspool 10 feet away. When I say that the bone-grinding department of a stockyard's plant is pleasant compared to the odor of the mixture contained in the cesspool, some idea will be had of the driver's condition when he was pulled out by Tompkins. In the meantime, Scotty was standing in the cookhouse, laughing his sides out at the driver's plight, and he had forgotten to notice that the mule was backing further and further into the room. Just then Mr. Mule got his foot tangled up in one of the dixies that were lying on the floor, and in attempting to kick it off, his foot missed Scotty's head by about six inches. Scotty backed up and so did the mule, still kicking, each kick bringing his hoof nearer Scotty's mug.

"Take your damn mule out," he roared, but they returned the laugh on him and made no move. The next kick brought the hoof and dixie within an inch of the cook's skull and in desperation and fear for his life he slid sidewise under the mule's belly and just escaped a vicious bite as he was getting out of the door.

What the mule did not do in that room to the dinner preparations was not worth doing and Scotty was peremptorily demoted for the loss of the men's dinner and put to tending mules instead. He had no more idea of caring for a mule than he had for performing a delicate operation on the brain and, as a consequence, when inspection day came around, the hip bones of the animals he had cared for could be

S.O.S. Stand to!

used as a hat rack and the officer ordered them shot and buried. The cook's thrift again came to the front. "Grant, I'll tell ye what I'll do, if ye'll help me take the carcasses to an abattoir we'll sell them for forty francs, and then we can dig a grave and let on we've buried them, and I'll go half wi' ye. What do you say?" The scheme looked plausible enough to me and I consented, and I was the richer by 20 francs.

Owing to his misfortune with the mules the O.C. ordered him to report for duty on my gun and Scotty came into the lines with us the following week. I was in charge of a trench mortar and our duty was to send over 8 or 10 shells, instantly take the gun to pieces and remove it to another position for the purpose of getting away from the return fire that Fritz was sure to send. When the first 10 messages were sent across, I ordered all hands to take their respective parts and carry them to the point designated, I superintending the dismemberment of the gun. When the last man, who happened to be Scotty, had taken away his respective part of the gun, I picked up the range-finder and started for the spot about a hundred yards off down the trench. I had scarcely gone 10 yards when an ear-splitting roar came hurtling through the air and an explosion followed that made the very earth tremble. I knew it was somewhere in the neighborhood of our selected spot and I anxiously hastened my steps. I got there to find every man of my gun crew with one exception blown to atoms, the exception being Scotty, but he too had paid the supreme price. With the help of another soldier, we carried him to the rear of the cookhouse and covered him with a blanket. When daylight broke I went over there with a party to give him as decent a burial as possible, and the new cook, who was a Scotchman, came out to have a look at the dead pal.

"Well, if it isn't Jock Henderson!" he exclaimed.

"Did you know him?" I asked.

"Know him! Why, mon, we were bakers taegither in Glascae. I could tell him anywhere by his bow-legs, an' he's got a scar on one o' them as big as your face."

"Yes, I know he has, where the shell grazed him at Mons."

S.O.S. Stand to!

"Shell grazed him at Mons? Shell hell! It was a pan o' hot dough that fell on his leg in the bake-shop, and I'll never forget his yell tae my dyin' day."

Like the last star of dawn the only remaining shred of poor Scotty's valor faded away and was gone.

S.O.S. Stand to!

CHAPTER XII
BEHEMOTH

The Somme district is composed of chalk pits; wherever the ground was dug up it showed white. This afforded an excellent opportunity for the enemy birds to spot any work we were doing. While in this section every man in the ranks looked very much like a white-wash artist—white dust everywhere, filling our eyes, ears, noses, mouths. Lord! when I think of that chalk dust!

For five days after the first advance of the tanks they were lying, six of them, immediately at the right of our battery on the edge of the road; no one seemed to know what they were doing there or what was contemplated. Then they moved up four miles to the edge of Pozières Woods, where they believed they would be safer from view, and for the further reason that they would not have so far to travel when the next drive was pulled off. They waddled in there at night, but the following morning Fritz's keen eye searched them out, wirelessed the necessary directions to their heaviest battery, and in almost less time than it takes to write it tremendous shells came smashing around, damaging one of them pretty severely, and the other five immediately waddled back to a safer place in the rear.

That same night canvas dummies were drawn up by mules and set up in the same place. Again the keen-eyed birds of the air spotted them, flashed their range back to their heaviest mouthpieces, and for the better part of the day the entire batteries of their heaviest caliber, expended their energies and their shells on the dummies; there was no kind or character of explosive shell that did not land on the frauds.

Late in the afternoon two of the air birds wanted to get down a little closer, undoubtedly to satisfy themselves as to how the work of destruction had progressed, and one of our little observation planes gave battle to the visitors, engaging the nearest one first. His companion bird made for ours, but before he could get underneath to do anything, the first German bird had been winged and downed. Our anti-aircraft guns now made it so warm for the other bird that

S.O.S. Stand to!

he beat it. The visit, however, must have had beneficial results for Fritz, for immediately after the plane returned to their lines, he ceased paying any attention whatever to the dummies. That night we put the real tanks behind the dummies and the day following not a single shell broke over or near them, and that same night they crept down into Pozières Valley under shelter of a bombardment made to prevent the keen ear of Fritz detecting the throbbing of their engines.

By this time batteries had been and were being installed everywhere at Pozières where there was room to place a gun: like beavers the men were working as busily as men could work, although they were constantly subjected to the severest strafing; but on the Somme it seemed that nobody minded. For my part I had the firm conviction that death would come when it would come and not till then, and I went about my work absolutely careless of any possible hurt. And I can positively testify to the same state of mind in each one of my comrades,—not one of whom seemed to think of his personal safety in any way whatsoever when there was work to be done.

Here the British soldier's fatalism was exemplified in the superbest manner!

On that same night that the tanks went forward again, I was detailed to go to the trenches to assist the telephonist, who was hard pressed for help, and in the morning I was in the front-line trench assisting the Captain with his observation work. All the time on the Somme all hands were busy doing something. Immediately after dawn, at five o'clock, the guns belched forth with an ear-splitting, deafening roar and simultaneously over the top appeared the five behemoths, one of them passing within a few feet of me.

The gunfire from our pieces at this time was immensely superior to the enemy's and his trenches had been flattened, but the wires still stood, and here it was the tanks did the work. On they came! Rolling through and making gaps 10 to 15 feet wide the Infantry plunging along in their wake. Forgetting my orders to stay where I was, I hopped in with the Infantry and reached Fritz' second-line trench.

"Gawd!" yelled a Tommy. "Wot the bloody 'ell will Fritz think of these beauties? 'E'll think its Satan's advance guard!"

S.O.S. Stand to!

On and yet on they reeled and rolled, one of them dipping nose first into a crater, and when I saw it going over the top of this huge hole my heart gave a bound of fear, as I surely thought its usefulness was now over. In this crater there were about 300 German soldiers when the tank plunged into it, and under its huge bulk 75 of them had their lives mashed out.

A spirit of wonderful fervor filled me as I saw that our behemoth was not disturbed in the slightest by the fact that he had gone into a crater; he continued to waddle all around the huge hole, his machine guns playing on the balance of the men that were jumping this way and that, and swarming like ants up, over and on top of it, to escape and save their lives in some manner. In sheer mad desperation they climbed over every part of the mammoth, discharging their revolvers at any seam in the metal or place where they thought it might be effective, breaking their bayonets on its iron coat—in vain! They could not overcome the unknown! One man thrust a hand grenade into the muzzle of one of the guns, but was blown to bits in the try. Still, over and over it they swarmed, like bees searching for a nook in a flower, the difference being that instead of getting honey they got hell. Then the poor desperate devils, in the frenzy of despair, flung themselves from the top and sides of the titan down into the crater and tried to scamper up the sides to the top, only to be met with a hail of bullets when they reached the edge and fall backwards into the crater depths, upsetting in their fall their companions who were behind them, and also trying vainly to get out of that hole of hell.

Language is futile to give anything like an adequate description of the scene in the crater. A few of the Huns, more long-headed than the rest, still clung to the tank, remaining there until it reached the top, when they held up their arms, yelling Kamerad at the top of their lungs, and these were all that were left of that 300—just 20.

The titanic ducks were each of them doing similar work on every part of the line, but the particular one whose work I was able to follow then made a call on a whiz-bang battery, smashing one of the guns when it first stepped upon it, and mowing the gunners down, the rest fleeing as though from the wrath to come. Many batteries and crews were similarly smashed, and then their work being done for the day, they all returned with the exception of one which lay in the German lines for about five hours, due to engine trouble. While lying there, Fritz did his damndest to place a mine underneath the helpless hulk, but the earnestness and the energy with which our boys at the guns worked for the preservation of their beloved behemoth, prevented him carrying out his purpose; and while the concert was in full swing all around us, the preserving messages from our guns whizzing past it in one direction, and the destructive messages from the German guns coming at it from the other direction, the tank crew quietly and industriously went about their work, repaired the engine trouble, said "ta-ta" to Fritz and waddled back home.

No returning hero from the scene of his glory ever received such a greeting as did the crews of the mighty monsters when they stepped out of the sheltering internals of their huge bowels. Clad in pants and boots, littered with grease, dirt and oil, scarred with bruises incurred as they were thrown from side to side of their armored shelter by the swaying of the thing, when they stepped from the door to the ground, the shouts and roaring cheers of ten thousand times ten thousand men thrilled them with such a thrill, that they felt fully repaid for everything that they had done that day.

The Tommies grabbed them in their arms, hugged them, slapped them on the backs and chests until the wind was fairly knocked out of them, and if we had been Frenchmen instead of Britishers, our mouths would have been covered with black grease from kisses imprinted on their cheeks.

All night long, long lines of men in gray were passing through our sector, in some places as many as 50 of them being escorted by one soldier; German Red Cross men were carrying out our wounded, eagerly volunteering for this work in the thought that they would find favor by so doing.

After taking Pozières and driving over the ridge and on down into the Courcelette Valley, we took up a position about 500 yards from the German front lines. Here occurred another of those remarkable

S.O.S. Stand to!

escapes from the Grim Reaper's toll that won for me throughout the unit the pseudonym, "Horseshoe Grant."

Eighteen loads of ammunition were being hauled to the guns and when being unloaded, enemy fire opened up on the position, several horses were hit, the doors of the wagons were flung open and the horses, stricken with fright, galloped madly about, the shells being strewn over the ground all the way to the bridge several hundred yards off,—a bridge that was a vitally important structure to us, because over it every pound of supplies and ammunition had to cross in order to get to us. I have often thought what a disaster it would have meant to us had Fritz ever got to this passageway. The drivers finally managed to close the wagon doors and get most of them back over the bridge, but the shell fire had then become so heavy that "Take cover!" was ordered.

The Hun kept up the bombardment for some time and the O.C. thought it better to let the ammunition lie where it was until daylight, when he intended to have it gathered up. He did not wait for daylight; in the middle of the night we were called out to manhandle the ammunition from an improvised sled that had been built and loaded with it and hauled over the mud to the bridge. There was no slacking on that job, every man carrying two of the shells—18 pounders—and when we finally got them to the guns we were allowed to turn in.

Behemoth in Battle

S.O.S. Stand to!

Just before daylight a counter attack started and we were ordered to repel it, which we did with all the ammunition that was capable of being used; lots of it we could not use as the mud and dirt prevented; it had to be thoroughly cleaned and oiled before being fired. The battle lasted well until noon, and having accomplished our work we got a "Stand down!" after which came the usual hurry and scurry to clean and oil our pet and get her all in readiness for the next act. There was still some ammunition left lying on the ground that had been spilled, and we were instructed to gather it in at once, clean and oil it and put it in the gun pit. While busy at this job I glanced overhead and noticed an airplane: "I believe that's a German," calling attention to it. The fellows didn't agree with me, they holding it was a British bird, and we all went on with our work. I kept my eye on it, however, for some reason, and saw it finally go over the ridge and turn, and as it turned—Kr-kr-kr-p! and a shell lit on the ridge 25 yards in our front; it was about an 8-incher and showered the dirt in all directions. We scurried like rabbits into our pit, emerging in a few minutes when the dirt and dust had blown away. Glancing up again I noticed the air bird turn again, and instantly another one came, this time landing near the gun pit, throwing a shower of mud and dirt on it, and causing considerable profanity for the extra work given us by Fritz. Instant orders were given us to take cover as a strafing was in sight, and we shot out of the gun pit, jumped into the trench and ran along. Two of the fellows were immediately ahead of me, Dinghy and Graham, and Graham's footwork was so slow that I jumped up on the parapet of the trench to get past him, and over the top I skedaddled toward our 30-foot dugout, which had formerly been the home of the Germans; like most of their quarters it was large, roomy and comfortable. To get to the dugout we had to go through a German gun pit which was then being used by us as a cookhouse. Just before I reached my destination a shell had landed squarely in this gun pit, where a number of the men were lined up waiting for supper. The effect of this shell was not only deadly in the extreme, but very peculiar in its action. At the right hand side corner of the gun pit was the dugout for the left section, and the right section occupied the dugout on the left hand side corner. The shell struck the edge of the right section dugout in which four men at the bottom were having a card game;

the fuse tore its way down the steps, knocking large chunks of the steps off in its course, and down into the center of the card game, scattering the money in every direction and not injuring a single member of the party. The back lash of the deadly visitor, however, ripped the life out of the men waiting for supper at the cookhouse and the side lash of its stroke caught the men in the right hand side dugout in which were two soldiers sitting on a box, munching biscuits. One of them had the upper half of his head blown off, scattering the blood and brains over his chum, who escaped without a scratch.

I reached the gun pit about one minute after the explosion. God in Heaven! What a sight met my eyes! The floor of the pit was strewn with the men in all directions, six of them dead and the balance fearfully wounded. I dashed out for stretcher bearers and Fritz just then started increasing his fire; he had kept an eye on the men running through the trench to the gun pit. He therefore knew that there must be a nest of us there.

In spite of the gain in the enemy's gunfire, we started our wounded pals to the officers' dugouts; most of the lads had been so severely shell-shocked that we had a most trying time to keep them in their stretchers. Men who have been shell-shocked most usually exhibit it by wanting to run off in all directions; I have seen them with wounds that ordinarily would cause them to collapse, but under the influence of the shock exert themselves with such strength and violence that it would take a couple of sturdy men to hold them. There is a trite saying that every disadvantage has a corresponding advantage and I wondered that night when I got back to the gun pit if nature intended that the advantage from this disaster was the increase in our supper ration due to the death and wounding of my soldier pals!

A few days after, we were notified we were going to drive forward another stage, and I went to the trench with the telephonist party for the purpose of making our communication as clear as possible; I was detailed especially to assist the Captain in this work.

The attack was launched at daybreak, with a ten-minute bombardment preceding, and then our fellows were up and over. As before, the tanks blazed the way, one of them passing about 30 feet

S.O.S. Stand to!

to my right just before I went over the top. As I lay in the trench, the darling old titan passed me, leveling the wire in front, and I had then an even keener realization of what it meant for Fritz to have these monsters piling over and smashing him under foot just about as a man would tread on a worm and mash it. And if there ever was one time during my entire three years of campaigning, when I felt an atom of sympathy for the gray-clad devils, it was at that moment.

But how can sympathy obtain for devils in human form?

My immediate family was strongly represented in this attack. To my right among the men who went over, were the Canadian Grenadier Guards, of which my young brother Billy was a member. This regiment had made an undying place in the annals of Canadian history in the advance on Courcelette, having out of its 950 men but 66 men left intact when the roll was called after the battle, the balance being either killed or wounded. But they achieved their objective, Courcelette!

Billy and his regiment, which had been mustered up to strength, passed over the top within four hundred yards of me to the right. On my left, my older brother, Gordon, who was supporting a trench mortar battery in the front-line trench, was working away within 500 yards of me. I was not aware of the presence of either until a comparison of notes later on apprised me of their presence. To my right hand was Hughey and his brother Archie and to my left Jim, three brothers, all of them my first cousins.

Jim had enlisted in New Zealand, Archie in Australia and Hughey in Canada. The only relative of whose presence in the battle I was aware, was Hughey. Through a rule obtaining in the army, these three brothers took the opportunity when they got to France, to get a transfer to the Canadian army, all in the same unit. Later, however, the casualties necessitated changing them around somewhat. All three had been wounded and gassed, but were back again as full of fight as ever. We went over under the shelter of such a terrific barrage that the German front line and its occupants were practically annihilated; the work of our artillery was nothing short of wonderful. Staying there ten minutes we went on and took the second line, meeting a little more stubborn resistance as we went forward, but finally taking it. In going over between the first and second lines it was necessary to jump into shell holes from time to time. The men ahead of us were mostly Brandenburgers, Bavarians and Prussians. At one place I had leapt with my pal into a small shell hole, and over to my right was a kiltie engaged in a hand-to-hand struggle with a Hun. The kiltie was an undersized chap and Fritz was about twice his size, and with a much longer bayonet, and Jock seemed to be getting a bit tired. I didn't think it wise to wait, even though I felt very certain that Jock could hold his own, and taking careful aim with my revolver I tumbled the Fritzie over. Looking then to the left I saw another kiltie in an argument with a Prussian; they were fencing with their bayonets, and a second Hun was coming up behind and again I took aim, but before I was able to get my pill started, my mate robbed me of the honor and sent his pill crashing through Fritzie's head. So I turned my attention to the immediate opponent, but before I could shoot, the kiltie's body interposed in my line of vision, and when I got a glimpse of the Prussian a second later, he was in the throes of death with a bayonet in his bowels. Further over to my right, two Huns were trying to bayonet a soldier, but our man was an expert and seemed to be easily holding his own, in fact, getting the better of it a little, and I noticed a Prussian jump out of a hole, aim his rifle at our fellow, and I yelled, "Get that one, Walter!" But Walter had already seen him and started blazing at him and winged him in the shoulder; he was later gathered in among the prisoners.

Then we turned to the duel and blazed at one of the Prussians, being lucky enough to land him, and at the same time Sandy got in his work with the cold steel on the other Hun. Then, wiping the perspiration from his face with a swipe of his hand, he looked toward us and hollered "Gude work, laddies," and dashed on ahead.

All these scrimmages took place in less time than it takes to tell about them; everywhere, as far as the eye could reach, the cleaning-up process was going on. This was as far as I could go at this time, because I had strict orders to remain with my party there for observation purposes, the Infantry going on ahead and taking the third line.

S.O.S. Stand to!

Resistance was growing more stubborn with the advent of each successive line, but they cleaned up and started for the fourth, and it fell. It was on that day that I understood the expression "Seeing red"; there was only one thought in my mind, kill! kill! kill! kill! The wave forged ahead for the fifth German line, taking it and smashing down all resistance in their way. They were in the middle of the cleaning-up process of the fifth line when the welcome sight of friend tank again hove in view, arousing cheers. They were needed just then.

S.O.S. Stand to!

CHAPTER XIII
THE FAMILY LUCK

At the fifth line the men stayed awhile, waiting for the word to take the sixth line, and our barrage was directed on this trench line so heavily, the Germans could not hold it. They left and our wave crossed over, but could not reach the much sought-for ditch, as a massed counter-attack drove them back. Our barrage again drove Fritz back, thus converting the sixth-line trench into a No Man's Land.

The Boche made a determined effort to retain it and counter-attacked time and time again, but each try met our machine guns, rifles and grenades, together with the barrage, and a distorted heap of dead Kaiserites was added to those already in this ditch of death.

Their ranks were getting woefully thin and pale; wave after wave came up in a bull-headed effort to keep the line, and, finally, to assist the fainting Prussians, a regiment of Brandenburgers jumped to their help, and again they came. By this time the trench was literally filled with dead, dying and wounded men. Over the Brandenburgers came, one thousand strong, right in the teeth of our barrage; in mass formation they charged, and it was impossible for a bullet to miss its billet in that line. They fell like flies on a tanglefoot sheet, and back they wavered into the trench. But there was no shelter for them there, as it had ceased to be an abiding place, because their dead and wounded comrades were piled in it clear up to the brink, and there was no place for them to stoop or crouch to escape the rain of death.

Our O.C. paused awhile to see what Fritz would do further, but—nothing stirring! So, over our fellows went. The corpse-filled trench offering no attraction for shelter, the wave rolled on to the seventh line, taking it and putting up there for the night.

A few hours later Fritz made a most determined attack on the seventh line, and sorry am I to tell that they made a little headway, taking some prisoners, among them being my cousin Jim; roll call the following morning also disclosed Archie as missing. For my dear

S.O.S. Stand to!

Auntie's sake it is my sincere prayer that he may yet be alive and well.

When the wave reached the first line in this drive, the trenches were filled with prisoners and orders were given to corral them in the different dugouts and rush them into the holes, but there was no need for hurrying them,—they were diving for them as fast as their legs would carry them. My brother Billy and a party was put in charge of a number of dugouts, Billy having one under his control. He did not know how many were in the dugout he guarded, but outside was a captured Prussian officer. The boys had now gone on ahead, leaving the prisoners' escorts posted here and there along the trench to guard them. This Prussian officer was standing a few feet away from Billy, on his right, and something diverting Bill's attention from him, the Prussian officer, in strict accordance with the Prussian code of honor, seized the opportunity, grabbed a rifle, and was about to plunge the bayonet into Billy, but he turned just in time to catch him in the act and avoid him. He lunged with his bayonet, catching the dastard in the left shoulder, and while tugging to get it out, the prisoners started rushing up the steps of the dugout, and Bill was forced to let go of the rifle; as he did so, the weight of the gun pulled the bayonet downward, ripping through the Prussian's black heart. Bill then took a bomb—he had eight of them—and let them go one after another into the dugout. Although fighting for his life, he knew if he faltered for a moment he would be lost, and he did not lose his head for a second; he realized that if he let any of these bombs leave his hand and reach the dugout in sufficient length of time before it exploded, they would seize them and hurl them back at him, or else escape this particular bunch who were trying to get him and who were strung on the steps leading down into the dugout. So, in the midst of the scrap he kept his nerve and his head, not letting a single bomb leave his hand until he was dead certain the time had expired and that the moment it struck the top step of the dugout, their mission of destruction would have been accomplished. This done, he yanked his rifle out of the officer's shoulder and jumped to the entrance of the pit for any others that might have escaped his fusillade of grenades. None came.

S.O.S. Stand to!

"Billy, take those prisoners out of the dugout," sang out the Sergeant-Major, "and get them to the rear, and tell the rest of the boys to do the same."

"I don't know how many are there, sir."

"I'll take a look and see," and the Sergeant-Major jumped into the dugout. In a moment he reappeared. "There are nine killed and three wounded. Round up these three and get them to the rear and get over the top as fast as you can."

Billy did so, catching up with his pals at the third line trench. When he got to the sixth line, a shell exploded in front of him, hitting him in the thigh and dislocating his hip bone, besides giving him a painful flesh wound. He was knocked unconscious and thrown into a shell hole. The hole was almost filled with water, but the horseshoe luck of the Grant family was with him; when he fell in his head was just out of the water.

There he lay for eight hours, when the moaning of a wounded pal, three or four feet away, roused him and he pulled himself over to him; his pal's leg had been shattered from the knee down and Billy, in spite of his own condition, managed to drag him for some distance toward the dressing station, hopping on his left foot as he went and then resting a bit. Finally the pain became too great and he could go no further; every nerve and fiber of his aching body was at the breaking point of utter exhaustion, and the pain of the gangrene in his wound, inspired by the mud and dirt, gave him his finishing touch and he dropped. Bill's pal then took up the struggle; he tottered to his sound foot and dragged him to the dressing station, where he dropped beside him.

The tremendous rush of wounded men waiting for treatment made it necessary for them to take their turn, and it was three-quarters of an hour before they could either of them get attention; the German wounded were treated in turn along with our own men, no favors being shown. This is in marked contradistinction to the untold and unspeakable brutality exercised upon our wounded prisoners in the German lines.

S.O.S. Stand to!

In due time they were carried to the rear by German prisoners, and then to England through the medium of the base hospitals and casualty clearing stations.

It is with pardonable pride I can say that they were not long in the hospital before they got word they were to receive a medal for their magnificent work.

Billy's splendid physical condition rapidly brought him through, although it was five months before he was really himself again, and he has since then gone back to the lines, where he was again wounded and in the hospital, and has again gone back and is still doing his bit.

On the following morning, I returned to the battery.

S.O.S. Stand to!

CHAPTER XIV
THE DEAD SHELL[1]

A late September mist, more hazy than foggy in its character, enveloped the line following a heavy deluge of nearly two days that had poured almost a foot of water in our trenches, and in some spots where holes had formed in the trench-bed the water came gurgling over the knee. On the whole, however, conditions were very much less worse than wading in the water up to one's waist, which was our common lot in the earlier days of the war. As one of our wags had it, "Mud under me, water around me and hell above me."

[1] *A dead shell is one that explodes at a predetermined time after it strikes—from one minute to several hours.*

For nearly a month Fritz had been inordinately busy with his "dead" shells; we had no rest from his activities. If there was an interval of time when we were not being served with the "dead" messages, the hiatus was filled with whiz-bangs and gas. Whichever his fancy dictated, for us it was the Devil's choice.

Following orders, under the friendly shelter of night's curtain, I was leading my squad to our gun positions in the front line, about three miles distant, and in slipping and sliding over the muddy ground, pitted with holes in such a manner as to suggest to one's mind that the earth's surface had been scourged with an attack of elephantine smallpox, we could not help chuckling, in spite of the discomforts of our journey, at the ejaculation of a Cockney Tommy: "Strike me pink, Sergeant, but Fritz would think we was his pals if he only saw this goose-step work." This was an allusion to the fashion we had to employ in picking our steps on the lookout for holes. In this region the fair face of nature is distorted in every conceivable way with holes and ditches, some of the holes big enough to engulf a house, and it is no mere desire to avoid the water in these holes that compels us to pick our steps in this hell-swept part of the world; it is the first law of nature, self preservation, for many a poor lad has been done to death in them by drowning.

S.O.S. Stand to!

On this night my squad, including myself, was composed of 13 men, and although none of the men, if they did notice it, mentioned the coincidence, I must confess, although I myself studiously refrained from making any comment about it, the thought of the fateful number kept recurring to my mind as we made our way to the spot where the visits of the Grim Reaper were so frequent that death had ceased to be anything but an every-day occurrence. It was only when some friend or chum paid the supreme price that we gave the matter any particular attention, and then it would be for but a short time. The necessity of every man's looking out for his own life gave him but little time to think of much else, unless, indeed, killing the Huns. Next to saving our own lives that is the heartfelt desire of each man—get Fritz. And yet, although the first thought of everyone is, naturally, for his own life, there is no history in this war that can be written that can recount the number of occasions when the seeming first thought of men was to do for their pals, utterly regardless of their own safety. For sheer toying with death and taking chances in situations that did not seem to offer the slightest hope or chance of getting through, the Great War discloses feats of valor with which nothing can compare that comes out of the mist of "Days of old when knights were bold."

After goose-stepping for over an hour, and almost completely winded, we flopped on the ground for a few minutes to catch our breath. We were within about half-a-mile of the ridge over which we had to go in order to get down into our dugouts, and Fritz' calling cards were commencing to come in our direction; star shells were shooting up at short intervals, the gleam of a flare every now and then plainly revealing ourselves to each other. As we sat there the conversation seemed to lag and a silence that struck me as somewhat ominous pervaded our little group. I wondered if the rest were thinking of our number. One of my best chums, Corporal Lawrence, was sitting next me, and I thought I heard him sigh.

"What's the matter, Corporal, winded?" I asked.

"No, no, Sergeant, I was just thinking."

"Thinking? Thinking of what? The cookhouse? I'll bet we are all thinking about that."

S.O.S. Stand to!

"No, Sergeant, it was not the cookhouse."

"Well, if it wasn't the cookhouse, is it that letter that is coming for you tonight?" said I.

"No, you are wrong, Sergeant; it wasn't either of those things, much as I would enjoy both the letter and the grub."

I felt that the gloom would become infectious if it were not immediately dissipated, and I blurted out, "Well, for God's sake, don't keep us all in suspense; how in hell are we going to go on until we know what you are thinking about?"

His answer made me sorry I spoke.

"I was just thinking," said he, "that my number is up."

This is an expression of the men on the Western Front when they have a premonition that their time on earth is short. A sudden fear smote me, but I banished the thought and started jollying him profanely.

"Now, Corporal, you know what damn nonsense it is to talk that way! Do you want to wish it on yourself?"

"No, Grant, I should say not, but I can't help thinking it, all the same."

"Yes, Lawrence," said McLean. "For God's sake don't wish any trouble on us more than we have got."

Billy McLean was my dearest pal; we had enlisted together and had formed one of those attachments that men sometimes make and is only severed by death, and we shared each other's most intimate thoughts. The words had scarcely died on McLean's lips when— Woo-o-f! Bang! Bang! and shells commenced to land all about us.

The spot we had selected to rest on was under observation; Fritz had evidently become aware of the fact that it was our usual course in coming to the trench and had registered the place for a target, just as he registered battery roads, ammunition depots, railway heads, sleeping quarters,—everywhere and anywhere that exhibited a trace of life immediately became an observation target and was subject to a hail of shell and shrapnel any hour of the day or night.

We were all slightly stunned by the dose, but recovered our senses in a minute or so.

"All right, fellows, let's be going," I said, and up we jumped, all except Lawrence.

"Come on, Corporal, finish your dream in the dugout." He made no reply. With a sickening at my heart I went over and put my hand on his face; it was wet with his life's blood; he was shot through the head. As hurriedly and as gently as possible we laid him in a hollow place and started for the ridge; we had no time for even a prayer, as we were being treated to a fair-sized fusillade, and ducking and dodging, this way and that, we made our way to the top as quickly as every ounce of energy left in our legs would permit, and rolled, tumbled, scrambled and fell—any old way—down the front side of the ridge into the ditch at the bottom, that was dignified by the high-sounding title of trench. It was as much a trench at that spot as any bog-hole. Its only virtue lay in the fact that if we crouched low enough into the water and mud we could escape the watchful eye of the enemy. We stumbled along through the inky blackness toward our gun positions, shrinking our anatomy to its smallest dimensions each time a flare shot up, and I was commencing to congratulate myself that we would reach our destination without any further hurt than the elimination of the thirteenth man;—I took a sort of sad comfort in the superstitious thought;—but we had still another target to pass. The Germans had made an observation point of a part of our ditch just a little bit farther along, and when we got to the spot we received a blast of shell fire that knocked us out of even our power to swear; we hadn't the strength; as a matter of fact, we were suffering with a slight shell shock. The dose consisted of about 200 shells, administered in quantities, first, of six at a time, then ten, then twenty-five.

One of the fellows nearest me again ventured the remark that he thought our number was up, and I just had enough vocal power left to curse him roundly for a damn fool. "You know what happened

S.O.S. Stand to!

Lawrence, don't you? Cheer up, you mutt! They will never get my number."

Throughout my three years' campaigning I persisted in repeating that "they would never get my number," until it almost became second nature with me, and the hairbreadth escapes I have had almost convinced me "there is something in it." Be that as it may, hundreds of men all around have "gone West" while I have been permitted to go through three years of it comparatively unscathed.

We finally got past the observed spot. The trench now commenced to run into a valley, and although there was water in it to a depth of fully two and a half feet, through which we had to wade, we were glad we were alive to paddle through it. But there was more trouble ahead. Fritz was turning gas into the valley, and I, being in front, got the first whiff.

"Masks, on with your masks," I roared, jamming on my own at the same moment. In addition to the gas, our friends had succeeded in shooting up a large ammunition dump, four hundred yards farther on, and the smoke and fumes from the exploding bombs, shells and other ammunition, to say nothing of the ear-splitting din, got me speculating as to whether our 13-squad was to go the way of so many reported thirteens. But my native optimism came to the rescue, and, with a curse, I drove the thought from me.

By this time our eyes were so blinded and stinging from the smoke of the ammunition fire that we were making our way almost by instinct, as we were half blinded, but the time-old provision of all things,—"Never a disadvantage without a corresponding advantage,"—came to our help. Under cover of the smoke we were practically secure from the shells and snipers, and stumbling and staggering round the fire, giving it a wide berth, we at last got to our gun position.

But, no rest! We had barely arrived when a delayed action shell battery opened up on us with a steadily-increasing fire, and, as the pace grew hotter every moment, I felt as if my nerves couldn't hold out longer; but the knowledge that these men were in my care helped me again to take hold of myself. But the rest of the fellows

S.O.S. Stand to!

were commencing to show signs of giving way to the shock effect. My best pal, Billy McLean, staggered toward me. "They've got my number, they've got my number," he shouted in my ear, and, beginning to give way to the shock, he fell at my feet, in the mud. I grabbed him and pulled him to his feet. "Cheer up, Billy, cheer up, old pal, how in hell are we going to pull through if you give way like this?"

"It's no use, Reg, they've got my number," and he moaned half hysterically as he leaned on me with an arm around my neck. Almost desperate, I shouted in his ear, "Billy, old pal, think of your mother and father; what would the old man say if he saw you acting like this? You know those hounds haven't a shell for either of us."

He roused himself: "I guess I haven't got the guts, Sergeant; I must be a damned coward."

"No, no, nothing of the kind, old fellow," I shouted, "but these boys are in my charge and I want you to help me play the game." He braced himself. "You're right, Sergeant, they haven't got our number and never will have." "Of course they won't," I answered reassuringly.

Poor Billy! His was a nature that was never intended for the business of killing; he was in constant dread and his nerves were always on edge when he was within shelling distance of the enemy, and he couldn't seem to shake off the terrible fear that was ever present except when in the top-notch excitement of going over; that was the only moment that he was able to throw off the blighting shadow that haunted him. Then indeed have I seen him throw the very first instincts of prudence to the winds and hurl himself into places where "angels fear to tread." But after the mad frenzy of the charge, with its accompaniment of shooting, stabbing, killing and maiming, he would collapse, and it would be some hours before he could regain his wonted composure.

The fire gradually slackened, our spirits began to revive, nature commenced to reassert herself, and we made our way to the cookhouse. We got our mess-tins filled with bread, cheese and jam, puddled our way to the dugout and fell to with the relish of healthy,

S.O.S. Stand to!

hungry, tired men who had fasted several hours. We gathered in the dugout occupied by Billy and myself. Feeling thoroughly rejuvenated, someone suggested a game to pass the time until mail arrived, and the well-worn deck was produced. Billy was sitting on my right hand and held cards that ought to have cleaned up, but he seemed to have lost the first instinct of a poker player, and I couldn't refrain from telling him he ought to confine himself to checkers. He whispered to me, "Reg, I can't get that out of my head." "What's that?" I asked.

"Fritz has my number; my time's nearly up and I know it." "Oh, hell!" I exclaimed, with a good-natured impatience, and giving him a poke in the ribs, "Forget it!"

The rest of the fellows chimed in with recollections of several fellows who persisted in saying that their number was up, and who were now pushing poppies, and the little Cockney murmured, "The poor beggars, and if they had kept their mouths shut they'd 'ave been with us yet."

It is a strange philosophy, but it is prevalent up and down the line.

At that moment the mail arrived, and Billy forgot his premonition for the time, for along with letters from his mother and sister, there was a photograph from his sweetheart that he showed me with suppressed joy.

"I say, fellows, what do you think of that for good time," said one, "my letters were both mailed on the 13th and this is only the 29th."

"That's a rum go," says the Cockney, "mine, too, was mailed on the 13th."

An examination of the mailing dates of our letters revealed the somewhat startling coincidence that every single letter we got that night had been mailed on the 13th. I mentally cursed the fateful number, but the news from home overshadowed the thought, as it did everything else, and I was careful to do everything I could to prevent its recurrence in the conversation. And, besides, the British soldier's fatalism, that death will come when it will come, prevented for long any gloom or oppressiveness in the atmosphere that might have been engendered by the time-old superstition. It was only in the exceptional cases when a soldier got into his head the premonition that his number was up that his spirits took a drop. I wish it were possible to convey in exact language the wonderful spirit of the men under circumstances and conditions endured by no soldiers in any other war since primeval man enforced his claims with his club.

Every man in the squad got letters and parcels that evening, and, all things considered, it was a happy bunch that left us to seek their bunks in their own dugouts. Billy and I remained up awhile after the others had gone, chatting about the home folks and, particularly, about his sweetheart, for at every opportunity he would turn the talk in her direction; he was positive there was no other girl quite so sweet as Aileen, for that was her name, and there was nothing for me to do but affirm everything he said.

"Reg, I want you to promise me one thing," said Billy, after we had been talking for an hour or more.

"What is it, Billy? You know I'll do it, old scout, if I can."

"Yes, I know you will. Well, it is this: I've told you how I came to correspond with Aileen, and, altho' I've never seen her yet, I really think she is one real girl. But here's the rub," he continued; "I don't really love the girl; I'm not such an idiot as to fall in love with a girl I have never seen; and you know lots of these photos are fifty per cent camouflage, ain't they?"

"You're dead right, old chap," I replied.

"Well, now, this one may be in the other fifty, and I'm thinking she is; and if you should get home before I do, will you look her up and let me know just exactly what you think of her?"

"Why, of course I will."

"That's what I wanted, Reg. You see, God only knows when I may get home, if I ever do, but I don't want to be nursing ideas about Aileen, and perhaps causing thoughts to arise in her mind, that may never be realized. You get me, Reg, don't you?"

S.O.S. Stand to!

"Surest thing, Billy, and you're damned right and sensible to look at it that way."

So that when we finally tumbled in, it was long after the witching hour of night.

The dugout we occupied we had built ourselves, and we took great pains to make it as roomy and comfortable as possible; hence the tendency of the fellows to make it their rendezvous. Our bunks consisted of sandbags spread out on the floor, and the ceremony of retiring occupied about one minute or less.

A half-muffled shriek woke me from a sound sleep and brought me bolt upright in the bunk. In the blackness I could just discern the outline of a man standing in the middle of the dugout and gulping as if trying to catch his breath. I jumped up and went to him. It was Billy. "What is it, Billy? What's the trouble?"

"Oh, Reg," he gasped, "I have had the most horrible dream!" He was shaking like an aspen. I put my arm around him and drew him over to my bunk. "Come, lie down with me, old man, and you will be as right as the rain in a minute." He laid down alongside of me and, still shivering, he recounted his dream to me.

"Do you remember that night I was telling you about when I was out observing?"

"Yes," I answered.

"Where we lost Thompson and the others when the flare went up? Well, you know that big Prussian I told you about, that came so near getting me? Do you know that fellow's face has never been out of my thoughts since I killed him, and I dreamed we were out there on that same spot again, and again the flare went up and we were rushed, and who should come at me but this man I had killed. I shrieked: 'You're dead! I killed you once. Get to hell out of here!' But he only gave a ghoulish grin and came at me. I dodged his blow and ran my bayonet through him, as I thought, but there he was coming at me again. Again I dodged and plunged into him, and again he was coming. Suddenly all power left me; my hands, arms and legs became nerveless, and I stood rooted; he clubbed his rifle, and as it crashed on my skull I awoke, and that must have been the time I cried out. And, Reg, just as sure as I am lying here, my number is up. I am as good as dead, I tell you."

"Now, don't talk such utter damn nonsense, Billy," I said, doing my utmost to comfort him.

"No damn nonsense about it. You know yourself we started out yesterday with thirteen men and Lawrence got it, and here tonight every letter we got was postmarked the thirteenth, and I just can't get it out of my nut, and I am not going to try any further."

"Billy, don't you want to live to get back home? Don't you know what it will mean to your mother and your father if anything happens to you? Well, what's the use of tempting fate? If it will come, it will come, and nothing you or I can do will prevent it; but there is something that helps a man—call it luck, or fate, or providence, or what you will—by keeping the idea firmly fixed in your mind that nothing can harm you."

I knew in my heart that nothing could prevent the dread messenger's visit when it was actually headed for one, still my philosophy had taught me that so far as I myself was concerned my determination to think positively about the matter had sustained me through many a trying moment when the fires of hell had surged about me, and up to that time I was as much alive as any man could wish to be, and I determined to stick to the philosophy, no matter how foolish it might seem when the cold light of logic played upon it.

A deep sigh was his answer. I continued for half an hour to encourage and jolly him, telling him that dreams always went by the contrary, and my efforts were rewarded by his growing calm and promising he would fight tooth and nail against the thought, and we finally dropped off to sleep.

"Show a leg, Grant, show a leg, cookhouse up," was yelled at me as daylight broke, and up we tumbled. I was much relieved that Billy was looking and acting as if nothing whatever disturbed him, except the possibility of being a second behind anybody else in getting to the cookhouse.

Although we were bosom friends and companions, there was just a shade of the big-brother idea on my part of the fellowship, and I kept track of him whenever and wherever I could. This was not alone because of the congenial soul that was within him, but, also, because I had learned through him to know his mother. And such a mother! It is a forward impetus on life's journey to know such a woman, and I knew instinctively she would expect me to keep an eye on him. And so, while I was fulfilling my duty, I had the double satisfaction of having combined with it the pleasure of association with a fellow whose tastes and ideals were absolutely akin to my own. There was no confidence we did not share; we laid bare our hearts to each other; in short, we were chums in every sense that the word implies.

Billy was ready for breakfast a second or two ahead of me, and he started up the steps, out through the door of the dugout. "I'm coming," I called, and grabbed my mess-tin and went up the steps two at a time. I reached the top and the door of the dugout, and, simultaneously, a roar and rush of air struck me, and I was thrown to the floor, stunned for the moment. My senses quickly recovered themselves, and I found my face and clothes dripping with blood. I commenced looking for my wound, but failed to find any. The discovery momentarily mystified me. It was blood, but whose? There was no report or explosion. A dead shell! A terrible fear took possession of me, and I shot up the steps into the trench. The Thing that met my eyes stilled my heart with a chill. The headless body of Billy lay at my feet. It was his life's blood that covered my face and clothes. A mist shrouded my brain for a moment, as I leaned against the side of the trench, utterly unable to speak or think. Then as the truth of the Thing worked its way into my brain, I glanced around for the cause. A large, jagged hole had been torn through in our front trench wall by a 300-pound shell, had snuffed out my pal's life in its course, and buried itself in the parados of the trench. There it was, the rear end of it just inside the outside edge of the hind trench wall, and when it exploded it meant death for any living thing within a radius of several yards.

S.O.S. Stand to!

Nature's primal law asserted itself and I dragged the remains of my best-loved friend several yards away and took from his pockets all his belongings and trinkets, and when I came to the photograph, partly stained with his heart's blood, hot, scalding tears blinded my eyes, and in deference to my dead friend's desire, I retained the photo, intending to get the news and picture back to her—in person, if possible. The O.C. took charge of the balance of his effects.

Disregarding all thought of my own peril from the unexploded shell which lay at the mouth of our dugout, I ran down the steps and got a blanket, in which I wrapped the poor headless body, and then reported to the O.C. and received orders to keep my men away from the spot for twelve hours. I hastened to the cookhouse and imparted the news to the men, as well as the orders. Heartfelt expressions of regret came from all, for in spite of his constitutional nervousness, Billy was a prime favorite. But I knew that I was the only one with whom the pain and sting would live; the men were so calloused by such happenings that they no longer made a lasting impression.

That was the longest and dreariest day I ever remember throughout my three years of campaigning. No thought of my turn coming entered my head, as I had so schooled myself into the belief that Fritz could not make a shell for me that I had long since ceased to give the matter any consideration whatsoever.

The day's work kept me from giving way to grief, and at nine o'clock that night, when in the cookhouse, I heard a whistle and someone shouted my name. It was our O.C., Major Wright. I hastened to his dugout.

"Sergeant Grant, I want you to take a party of six and make a grave and bury poor McLean. I know something of the relationship that existed between you, and I know that you will spare no effort to see that he is properly buried. While you are working I will try and fashion a cross for him. Report as soon as you are finished."

"Yes, sir," and I saluted and went to the dugout occupied by my squad. The men were either reading or writing letters, and not only the six, but the ten of them responded, dropping their letters and books, and asked to take part in the burial. So we paddled through

S.O.S. Stand to!

the darkness and the mud to where the body lay, and as we approached we noticed several huge rats scurrying away from it. A hatred for the vermin almost as intense as for the Hun has possessed me ever since. Of course, the bestiality of the latter has descended to such depths of infamy that it is impossible quite to class them with any other breed of vermin; it would be an insult even to the rat.

We dug the grave as well as we could, assisted by such light as we got from the intermittent flashes of the guns and the edge of the flare gleams sent up by the enemy every little while. When the melancholy work was almost complete, I hurried over to the O.C. and he handed me the simple cross he had made, — just two pieces of wood with the inscription, "William McLean, C.E.F., September 30th, 1916, R.I.P."

"When you have finished, Grant, take the party and build up the part of your trench that was shot away this morning."

I saluted and returned to the grave. The boys had finished; there was nothing more on earth we could do for Billy.

"O.C. says to build up the hole in the trench that was shot away this morning; you can go, fellows; get busy and I will be with you in a minute." They started and I was alone. Bitter tears again half blinded me as I placed the sign of the Christ at the grave's head; I couldn't place it at Billy's, because the shell had obliterated all traces of his head. With a short but very earnest prayer that God would help his mother and dear ones to sustain their loss and soften their grief, I hurriedly rejoined my men. On the way over I could not help thinking how lonely it would be that night in the dugout without Billy, and memories of the hundred and one incidents connected with our toil and trouble and joy in fixing up our nest flocked through my tired mind.

They were hard at work mending the damage done at daybreak by that messenger of hell. As I reached the spot, one of the boys remarked, "If that shell explodes before we get through, there will be no need of a grave for us." Very nearly fifteen hours had passed, however, since it had struck, and none of us felt there was any danger from that direction, as it was quite uncommon for any of them to burst if they had not done so within at least twelve hours, and I answered, "Oh, no, fellows, there is nothing to fear from it." I stepped to the back of the trench where the shell was imbedded in the parados and examined the spot. "I guess it is there for keeps," I said, and returned to work. In a few minutes one or two of the boys complained of thirst, and I volunteered to get water. I ran down the steps into my dugout, got Billy's water bottle and my own, and doubled down to the cook's dugout, filled them with drinking water, and was just starting back when the ground under me shook with an explosion, splinters coming from all directions, and one of them slightly wounding the cook. I thought at first Fritz had struck an ammunition depot, so tremendous was the roar. I grabbed the bottles and shot back to my party.

They did not need the water; they had been swept into eternity by the dead shell, and I was the sole surviving man of the thirteen-squad that I had taken into the line the night before.

CHAPTER XV
SATAN'S SHELLS AND SCENTED GAS

Prior to an attack in the morning, we cleaned up the gun and ammunition, getting everything in shape and retiring at 11:30. "Stand to!" was called at four o'clock, firing commenced at 4:30, and we worked our guns for two hours, during which time the boys went over, took three lines of trenches from Fritz and in a remarkably short time, hundreds of prisoners were turning into our lines without escort.

That night the prisoners were employed going up and down our lines carrying out wounded. I shall never forget the contented look on the faces of these captives as they worked inside our lines; they did everything required of them with a willingness and cheerfulness that at first seemed to be amazing. Most of them were young Bavarians and presented a very shabby appearance.

We then decreased our rate of fire, letting go one round every two minutes, giving us time to sit around and chat about the big surprise we had given Fritz and the success of our attack. Before giving the word to fire I would first warn the men, so they could look out for their eardrums, besides getting out of the way; we never fire unknowingly to any of the men as the concussion works a severe hardship on the ears. One of the boys was sitting on an ammunition box, leaning against the gun wheel, with his feet on a little fireplace that we had taken a chance on installing, thinking the fog was so thick Fritz would not notice the smoke. As usual, our ammunition was stationed in our rear. One fellow was squatting on the sand bags and leaning against the shells; I was sitting in seat three, between the gun wheel and the left side, while another was on seat four, also between the gun wheel and the gun on the right; another man was standing ready to put a shell in the muzzle.

"Fellows, are you ready?" I asked.

"All right."

"Fire!"

S.O.S. Stand to!

The next instant I felt my feet giving way from under me. The gun had blown off at the shield, the muzzle being blown to pieces, gas and fumes filled the air, the spokes were blown out of the wheels, splinters striking me on the feet and legs. I started to the front of the gun and fell on top of Graham.

"What happened?" he asked. "I don't know," I said. There were several pieces of tube lying about that looked like parts of a German shell. Graham yelled to know what had happened. "A German shell hit the gun," I said. He was then seized with shell shock and became uncontrollable. Park, who was leaning against the ammunition, was blown up, the shell having driven clean through his spine; the man loading the shell had a fragment driven clear through his stomach. The man leaning against the gun wheel was beheaded as cleanly as any king's executioner with his ax could do it, his head lying in the fireplace! The cartridge had exploded but the shell did not.

The trouble was caused by what is known as a "defective" shell.

I left the gun pit to help Graham over to the dressing station and I had a job on my hands; he was suffering from a bad attack of brain concussion. After attention a couple of Fritzies carried him to the rear.

Returning to the gun pit I found a state of wild confusion among the fellows as to what had really happened. On examination I found it was this defective shell; over to the right of the gun I picked up a chunk of it over a foot long.

Those who remained of our gun crew went that night to the wagon lines, spending a few days there while waiting for our gun to be replaced.

When our gun was replaced I started back from the wagon lines, carrying a piston rod of the buffer, with Downey assisting me. We were on horseback and getting into Labazell Valley, when a shell passed over our head so close that we felt the wind of it; it was accompanied by a great flare over to our right. The shell struck one of our ammunition dumps containing about 50,000 rounds of shells and other explosives, such as rifle grenades, Mills bombs, French

S.O.S. Stand to!

mortar bombs, aerial torpedoes, high explosive shells, shrapnel shells, star and gas shells. The disaster resulting from this one single shell was almost inconceivable. It started a fire that gathered strength each second, for all the world like a prairie fire, and the scenic effect was that of a titanic fireworks exhibition. The moon was brightly shining in a clear sky, but the star shells shooting in the air and exploding with a constantly increasing rapidity, the blaze of artificial light quickly obtained ascendency over the mistress of the night; and the shrapnel shells, throwing their contents of danger in all directions, together with the hissing and roaring of all the other exploding missiles of death, formed a diapason of sound that makes one of those wonder-moments that come so seldom in a lifetime.

The reflection of the fire from the explosion was quickly observed by Fritz, and in short order he had his airplanes hovering overhead, and they too were dropping their bombs wherever human activities were noted. We hastily dismounted, tying our horses to the barbed-wire iron pickets in the side of the road, and rushed with a body of men, mostly wagon drivers whose wagons were stalled on the road in the congestion, over to do what we could to save the ammunition which is so badly needed at all times.

In the first rush toward the pile an explosion snuffed out the lives of thirty or forty of the men, knocking the rest of us off our feet like so many nine-pins, besides killing several of the horses on the road, and to add to the already indescribable chaos, several of the horses stampeded, racing blindly into barbed-wire entanglements and adding to the general destruction.

What with Fritz dropping bombs from his airplanes, our horses stampeding and screaming like wild things, and our own explosives bursting in every conceivable direction with a thousand different roars, the scene can be better imagined than described. We saved about 10,000 rounds out of that entire dump. For a distance of twenty miles the reflection of the fire extended, the rockets themselves being visible for a space of ten miles. I don't suppose since the world began was there ever a scene of such awful beauty; it was a bursting Vesuvius with the co-mingled radiant beauties of a thousand rainbows.

S.O.S. Stand to!

When there was nothing further that we could do, we regained our frightened mounts and resumed our journey. Such a road of confusion! The ground being wet, turning the chalky earth into white, the moving, wriggling vehicles of every kind and description afforded a magnificent target for the marksmen of the air and casualties here, there and everywhere along the road was the order of the night.

A short distance along, the sounds of battle in the air reached our ears, and looking up I saw two shadows passing between our eyes and moon, then two more. Suddenly our searchlights opened up, and there, in full view, were four planes, two British and two German, engaged in one of those struggles which practically forms the only feature in this war around which is thrown any of the elements of romance that appeals to all the instinct of a vivid imagination. It was a fair field and no favor. The battle had been on about three or four minutes when one of the British birds landed on Fritz, driving him down nose first. He could not regain control and he dashed headlong into the earth to destruction. Our fellow then rose and went to the assistance of his pal and they made short work of the second Taube.

That is the only time I have ever witnessed a scene of that kind under those circumstances, and it is a rare occurrence indeed that one has the privilege of seeing such a struggle with such a background.

We were now among the batteries; to the right and left of us the guns had commenced speaking to the German roads, and the ammunition dumps there, in retaliation for the destruction of our gun-food; the anti-aircraft guns were also getting into the chorus, together with the pom-poms, and the whole swelled into a mighty chorus of sound that filled every crack and crevice in the air, making one feel as if he were inhaling sound rather than ozone.

As we neared Pozières a 9.02 howitzer gun on our left fired a shell that exploded in the gun and blew the gun and crew in all directions. The shell also started some ammunition going that was lying about and it was under the greatest difficulty that the men, whose lives were not lost in the first explosion, managed to get away. The men

S.O.S. Stand to!

were trying to manhandle the remainder of the guns of the battery and we jumped off our horses, fastened them to an old wagon lying in the ditch, and headed over to lend a hand. With much tugging and perspiring we saved three of the guns.

Explosions of these tremendous projectiles were deafening in the extreme, and here there were two or three of them exploding at once in our immediate neighborhood.

Again we mounted on our way to Pozières and, when reaching our journey's end, Fritzie began pumping in his crying shells; these are the kind that draw copious tears, inflame the eyes and make things generally disagreeable. We had not brought our goggles and suffered from a temporary spell of blindness; we had not had any trouble from this particular kind of visitor for some time and had not bothered to keep our glasses with us. Groping along, blinking my eyes to get a little gleam of light, I stumbled across four or five dead horses and was nearly thrown from my horse.

I warned Downey, who was behind me, and he avoided the trouble, but we had to keep a tight rein on our thoroughly frightened animals. It was impossible to get them past the dead horses until some others went by and then, leading them by the bridle, we got by.

Traffic was now fearfully congested on account of some tanks that were taking cover in the sunken road for their attack in the morning, and a shower of shells dropping here and there along the road did not add to our comfort. We passed through Courcelette Valley and came to a small bridge crossing a trench; this particular bridge was the subject of hot shellfire, as it was the only point where traffic could cross for about a mile to the right or left, and Fritz was well aware of the fact. When half-way across, a shell exploded, killing my horse, and the animal rolled over with me on its back, twisting my leg. For a while I thought my number was up; in a few moments I was able to get up behind Downey.

We had reached the end of our journey, got to the gun, delivered the piston rod and reported to the Captain. He instructed us to stay there for the night and told Downey to tie up his horse in one of the

S.O.S. Stand to!

German gun pits; then Downey was ordered to go on S.O.S. sentry duty. He had our sincere sympathy, for the rest of us were just breaking into the little old game for the balance of the night (morning).

In the middle of the game Downey came running in. "Say, fellows, there's a hell of a smell out here,—something sweet, never smelt it before, don't know what it is." "It's gas," I yelled, "the new kind! Get on your masks!"

We adjusted our protectors and made for the entrance. Downey began to be overcome by the fumes and I took over sentry; the warning gas horns were booming up and down the line like a deep-throated buzzing,—a most unearthly and weird sound.

The gas shells were now dropping plenteously round about and one of my pals, Dory, was instructed to assist me in relighting our lamps, as they were growing dim; these are our feed lamps that are lit every night with candles and placed, one for each gun, about 50 feet in front, and on these lights the sights are trained, so that it is vital to keep them burning all night long.

We rapidly commenced replacing the burnt-out candles, and just then we heard the warning roar of a coming shell, but before it burst I heard a splash; it was Dory taking a header into a shell hole full of water; I threw myself flat. In adjusting our lamps we had to remove our gas helmets, and after waiting some time for the expected explosion and hearing none, I looked up; white fumes were rising from the ground at about the spot the shell had entered; there had been no explosion of splinters.

This particular shell is very thin, is fired with great velocity, and when meeting resistance it breaks and cracks and the white gas fumes like steam come floating out. "What do you think of that, Grant!" from Dory in the shell hole; "I thought the blankety-blank was a Jack Johnson." His thought had cost him a soaking and the reflex action of his thought was strongly in evidence during the balance of our watch.

S.O.S. Stand to!

The remainder of our lonely duty was not enhanced in pleasure by the contemplation of scores of stretcher bearers carrying out men who had been caught unprepared by the gas and who were choking and suffocating from its effects.

So earnestly pernicious is the gas device as a fighting weapon that it is a matter of common talk among the boys that Fritz, when he invented his contrivance, must have been in direct communication with his Satanic Majesty.

Working tooth and nail to smother the Hun, and he in turn working might and main to smother us, was the order of the day continuously throughout the campaign on the Somme, and a few nights following the happening above, Dory and myself were on S.O.S. sentry.

About 3:00 o'clock A.M. the messages from Germany started coming and our replies were mailed back as fast as the postal authorities at the guns could handle the matter; in fact, throughout our campaign on the Somme we mailed our replies and our additional messages so rapidly and so effectively, that nine times out of ten Fritzie's working force was swamped.

On this A.M. his shells were gas which glazed the feed lamps and the sight of the lenses, as well as accumulating in the inside of the gun muzzle, making it necessary to swab out the muzzle of the gun before using, as otherwise it would rust badly, which would result in putting the gun out of commission in short order. The fire developed into a first-class artillery duel, our battery and nine others answering ten German batteries. The net result of the duel was two of Fritzie's guns put out of business.

Before long our lamps on the sandbags, by which we got our light to see to work the guns, were knocked off by an explosion and we were in darkness; following that, the springs in the buffer of my gun were broken, making it necessary to put it back in place by hand. Each time the gun is fired it recoils and is brought back to place by the hydraulic buffer containing the spring; but we had to perform this work in the darkness by hand. The coals of Hades were now coming in heavier each moment, because heavier caliber pieces had opened

S.O.S. Stand to!

up on us, and we were getting the worst of it; our weightier sisters must take a hand at the game, and we kept up our end of the argument until this could be done.

It was Dory's duty to reload the gun and push it forward in place for position, each time yelling "Ready!" One time the gun was shoved into place and the man on the right,—Dory was on the left—gave the "Ready!" and I fired. The darkness was still thick and I could not see that Dory was pushing up on the gun with all his might, to bring it into place when I fired, and the recoil drove him back into the corner against a pile of ammunition, smashing his arm. We assisted him, and one of the fellows volunteered to go with him to the dressing station, but Dory was game to the core; he was one of the most happy-go-lucky boys I ever met. "Hell! I will make it myself. Stay here while the fun is on. I wish to God I could stay too!"

We renewed our duel, but the heavier caliber shells were commencing to tell; number 3 gun was struck and part of the crew wiped out. Our telephonist 'phoned headquarters for the weightier women to get busy, telling them of our plight, and inside six minutes the ladies of larger girth, the 9.02 howitzers, started debating the question with Fritzie so vigorously that inside of thirty minutes not a single reply was to be had from their guns.

"Stand down!"—and cleaning our guns, gun pits and carrying ammunition, busied us. In the midst of our work a dizziness seized my head, accompanied with a choking in the throat and lungs, and before I could cry out or warn my pals, I dropped. I had unconsciously imbibed the potion when I removed my mask to relight the feed lamps, and it is one of the peculiar effects of this dose that it is some time after its inhalation that the harmfulness becomes apparent;—so it was with me. I was lifted onto a stretcher and carried to the dressing station near what is known as the Sunken Road. The ground around the station was dotted with men suffering from attacks of a similar nature; there were 56 of us in all.

The doctor's examination was brief,—"Gas," and I was laid alongside my brothers in misery. We were ordered to keep absolutely quiet and on no account to leave our stretchers; but while lying there the unwelcome messages from the German guns began coming in our neighborhood; and the ever terrifying sound of their explosions brought the nerves of the men, already on edge, over the border line of reason, and a number of them struggled up from their cots and started running away, forgetting or ignoring the doctor's orders. The poor fellows paid dearly for it; some of them dropped in their tracks, dying, where they dropped; some died after they were brought back to the station, and some gave up the ghost when in England they lost the last remaining tissue of their lungs, due to the effect of their running. "I mustn't budge!" I kept repeating to myself, for my own nerves were at the jumping-off point and I thought the veins in my head would burst if I had to endure those explosion-roars another minute. Happily they ceased as suddenly as they began.

There is no kind of suffering endured in the battle front that has such a horror for the men as the gas; it is that fighting for breath that takes the life out of a fellow, and, God! how it chokes. Out of that bunch of 56 gassed men, only six came out whole.

The following week we were ordered to leave the Somme. Although I felt in the mood for sticking it as long as I had the strength to keep going, yet I must confess the order filled my soul with a gratitude that was unspeakable. I had been in the Somme campaign three months, and when our guns swept into position at Martinsaart, my weight was 171; when I left, I tipped the scales at 145. The men who had been with the guns there and who know what it is to work 24 hours in the day for many days in the week, rarely during the three months experiencing the refreshing rest of a consecutive two hours' sleep, and working like veritable demons during every waking moment, either at the guns or cleaning the ammunition, or carrying the ammunition into place,—they will understand what it means to lose 25 pounds in weight on the Somme.

My uniform was in rags and saturated so thickly with grease and dirt that for many days it was one of my pet recreations to take a knife and scoop it by the bladeful out of the khaki cloth. And my skin! What a hide! The combination of cleaning and repairing guns, working them constantly, driving horses, observation work, together with the gas, my body was saturated with a mixture that took weeks to extract.

The cut-up-ground, pock-marked with shell holes as closely as the cells in a honeycomb, was of course carefully noted by Fritzie's aerial observers, and they were naturally led to believe that it would be physically impossible for our batteries to be relieved,—that is, to retire and another battery take our place. But we camouflaged. Under cover of a fog we worked like beavers for a day and a night, filling in shell holes, and made fairly decent roads under the conditions, and one fine morning, still under the friendly shelter of the fog, leaving our ammunition behind, we pulled out the gun; the entire Canadian Division retired and were relieved by the English Tommies.

As we were going out we passed their batteries coming in and it was heartening indeed to hear the compliments and praises that were showered upon us by the lads of England, although we had not done a single thing that they could not have done and done just as well as we, and maybe better.

In some places where our guns were stationed the ground conditions made it absolutely impossible to remove them for the time; in such cases the Imperial batteries left their guns at the horse lines and took over the Canadian guns, the Canadian gunners taking their pets instead. This occasioned a real and heartfelt loss to both Canadian gunners and Imperial boys who had to change over their pets, because every gunner learns to acquire a real affection for his mistress, as he terms the gun, and with many of the men it was like losing a good horse or a dog to whom they had become sincerely and warmly attached, the attachment being born of weeks and months of the most arduous trial and test.

We reached the wagon lines with our guns still intact and we felt as safe as if we were back in our beloved Dominion. We were going back of the lines, and the scene of breaking camp in our preparations for returning to the rear was picturesque in the extreme. Bonfires made of refuse and waste material for which we had no further use were burning everywhere; men were hurrying hither and thither; and through it all you could hear the steady digging, shoveling and

S.O.S. Stand to!

pounding of the German prisoners who were repairing the roads their own guns mangled. I felt a large measure of satisfaction at seeing them working as hard as they could go, restoring at least that much of their destructiveness; they will never, they can never replace the wantonness, the frightfulness, of which they have been the inspired tool in this the struggle of their lords and masters for the earth's control.

Night and day for three days we traveled on our batteries, arriving at a place called Camblain-Châtillon, a small town in a mining valley. Here we were billeted in barns, but the inhabitants hearing that we were Canadians who had been operating on the Somme, came out *en masse* to greet us and give us of their best. We were invited to their homes, and their larders were placed at our disposal; a large bath made of granite—a splendid outfit used by the miners of the town, was thrown open to us, and it is needless to say we reveled in the luxury of a plunge as quickly as we could tumble in. How we needed it! I had not known a bath during all the time I was on the Somme and lousiness was part and parcel of my make-up. I was so accustomed to it, however, that it had long ceased to cause me more than a passing thought; there were too many other things to think about during that session. But once relieved from the tension of the daily struggle to save life, as well as take it, the desire to become normal, decent, cleanly human beings took possession of every man of us, and we wallowed in the bath until we could once more look other respectable citizens in the face.

In this haven of rest and retirement we luxuriated for two weeks, then moved into action on the Lens-Arras road. We placed our guns on the side of the road, digging our trails in the edge of the cobble stone pavement as a trail block, to hold the guns steady when firing. Chicken wire on top, covered with grass and brushwood, completed the scenic protection.

Our work was the well-known ruse of a night raid in preparation for the attack on Vimy Ridge, and carried out for the purpose of keeping the Germans guessing as to where the next drive would be driven.

Leaving four men and the telephonist with the guns that night, we went to Anges, half a mile from the gun position, to our billets; this was an old French château, and comfortable beyond expression. As the foes of our anatomies had again attacked in mass formation, this time we were annoyed to a degree. Procuring creolin, we rubbed it on our bodies pure; it should have been adulterated. During the night the natural perspiration of our bodies caused the vermin grease to work through the pores, and excessive stinging and smarting was the outcome. One fellow awoke with a grunt of impatience and then a snort of anger, as a sense of the stinging brought him to a realization of his discomfort; then another, and another, until the entire bunch was in a fine frenzy, fanning our bodies and running into the night air for relief. My carcass was on fire and I wished to heaven I had left the lice alone; they could not at least have prevented my sleeping. I determined for the future, as against this cure, I would keep the curse. I felt as if I were suffering from a severe sunburn over every inch of my body.

A First Line Hospital

In the midst of our misery "Stand to!" was sounded, necessitating the dropping of all our skin troubles and skedaddling to get to the guns. We ran across an open field that had been converted into a graveyard after the French drove the Germans over on to Vimy Ridge, but there was no thought of sacrilege in our minds as we raced pell-mell over the grave-filled land; there never is but one thought in our minds; we are, every man of us, souls with but a single thought when "Stand to!" sounds. We reached the guns

S.O.S. Stand to!

practically in the nude, and fastening the sights and scratching my hide at the same time kept me fairly busy.

We worked the guns for an hour; then "Ammunition up!" was the order for the rest of the night. We were not allowed to return to our billets as another attack was expected. At 5:30 the first snowstorm of the winter swept over the land. The ground was fairly firm from the preceding frost, and in a short time the country was resting underneath a mantle of beautiful purity. With the enthusiastic ardor of a lot of school boys, we grabbed up the beautiful element in our hands and an old time snowball fight took place. Then the "Stand to!" of the morning was given.

Our objective this time was to cut channels through the wire about 15 to 20 feet wide, to permit the infantry to pass. This work is effected by means of shrapnel shells that cut the wire into little strands, then high explosives are used to root out the remaining posts. When we had accomplished our purpose and made everything ready for the charge, "Stand down!" was sounded. The infantry took up the program and dashed over and through the gaps we had made. They cleaned up the first line, then on to the second, smashing their guns, trench mortars and trenches, bombed the dugouts, destroyed their rations and sent back over 1800 prisoners. What I call a fair morning's work!

Now, as I have heretofore said, the objects most easily seen by an airplane are white and black and the surface of the earth being covered with a mantle of snow, naturally the things that the keen-sighted airbirds would first look for would be dark-colored.

The snow around our battery by this time had been thoroughly melted by the heat from our guns—as a matter of fact, the guns were steaming—and one of our Sergeants, knowing how easily discernible our pieces would be to the enemy airbirds, began gathering snow and spreading it all over the places where it had melted. He was working hard throwing the snow immediately in front of my gun when another "Stand to!" came. Let me repeat, if I have not already made it entirely clear, that when this most imperative order is sounded, there is only one thought in the mind of every man of the battery, to get our message off as quickly as human power can send it; and throughout every stage of the world's work that we are doing over there, there is no time when the bodies of men are entirely free of bruises received in collision with one another in the absorbing endeavor of every man to respond. This will account for the lamentable accident that occurred at this time.

The Sergeant, unthinkingly, after "Stand to!" was sounded, went on in his earnest endeavor to camouflage the battery with the snow. Now it so happened that at the identical time that the Sergeant was so engaged, a kiltie battalion was making its way to the trenches on a foot path, running diagonally across the front of the guns. In obedience to the command to fire, the crew speeded to their respective guns, jammed back the levers and the missiles started on their journey of destruction. The shell from our gun in front of which the Sergeant was working killed him before he knew what had happened and, as luck or the devil would have it, the shell was a premature; it exploded at the point of the muzzle and its 365 shrapnel pellets, each traveling at the rate of 2200 feet per second muzzle velocity, and which when exploded assume the shape of a gigantic fan, shot death and destruction into the kiltie battalion in front. Sixty of the kilties paid with their lives the price of this premature shell, including the Sergeant. For a hundred yards in every direction the heads, arms and legs of the Scotch fighting men were strewn all over the ground. It was one of those terrible things that is a matter for the deepest concern and regret, and yet cannot be helped.

We were next ordered back to the wagon lines at Camblain-Châtillon, arriving there on the evening of the 23rd of December, and preparations for Christmas dinner were uppermost in the mind of every man. We were delighted by a visit from the town authorities who asked us if we would like to use the schoolhouse for our celebration and that we were most heartily welcome to it, which offer we were most heartily glad to accept, and the authorities proceeded at once to decorate the schoolhouse in true holiday fashion, evergreens and lanterns filling every nook and corner of the large room. The tables, of course, we supplied ourselves.

S.O.S. Stand to!

For turkey we had a French pig purchased from a farmer for 300 francs, each man chipping in three francs; new carrots, Irish potatoes, boiled onions, cranberry sauce, the latter supplied by a large-hearted French lady in the town, made up the accompaniment of the "Turkey." For dessert we had a speech from Major Wright, congratulating us on our work in the Somme. In a few well-chosen words he told us how we had lost over 60 per cent of our men, counting the reinforcements, and that it was a matter of sincere gratitude to every man of us that we were there to enjoy the bounteous Christmas cheer.

CHAPTER XVI
BEFORE VIMY

In the course of ten days we arrived at Bully-Grenay, situated in the very heart of the mining district, three mines being located in the town itself. We were still working on the Vimy Ridge proposition. At no time in France were our quarters more comfortable than here; each gun of my battery was stationed in the cellar of a private house on the outskirts of the town from which the civilians had been shelled, and at night in the midst of a game of cards, or engaged in our letter writing, or reading, when we got the "S.O.S." signal, the lanyard was at my hand and I had only to pull the rope. Our quarters were heated by coal purchased direct from the mine and furnished to us at ten cents per bag. Every mine in this place was worked only at night, the smoke of the industry indicating to Fritz where to plant his shells; therefore, the entire coal mining was done during the hours of sleep.

The Huns were making a most determined effort to get possession of Bully-Grenay and these most valuable coal mines, and they were anxiously looking forward to the time when they could attack successfully, and knowing how vital to us it was to get out this coal, they concentrated their efforts through the daytime on the mine shafts in an effort to destroy them; but having no smoke signals to guide their fire, their efforts generally were futile.

A notable instance of the spirit controlling our ideas of warfare was splendidly illustrated in this particular sector. Among the captured French mines that the Germans were working was one in close proximity to a church, of whose existence they took particular pains to let us know; and the church, in addition to being used as a protection for the mine, was also used as a camouflage for one of their batteries, the guns being placed immediately in front of it. It is repugnant to the very soul of a British soldier to level his gun at a church, so Fritz was able to get away with his camouflage.

On the morning of the third day of our visit here we were treated to another superb example of *kultur*. The school children were playing

S.O.S. Stand to!

in the school yard and Fritz dropped a shell in their midst, killing and wounding several, following it up by two others that smashed the schoolhouse. A panic followed among the teachers and children, and the only thing we could do at the time was to stand there and watch the devilishness. Some of the men of an infantry battalion who were billeted on the outskirts of the town, rushed to the school and carried out the wounded and dead. If Fritz could have seen and heard the maddened fury of those rescuers as they carried out the maimed and bleeding little ones, his first thought would have been to have given them as wide a berth as possible; but when they did meet,—God help them!

At 1:00 o'clock in the morning Fritz opened up with gas shells, smothering the civilian population, and the people who were running out of the town, choking and suffocating, brought to my mind a most vivid recollection of the city of Ypres. How can I describe the agony, the despair on the faces of the inoffending citizens who were having their homes blasted to bits, their lungs choked with suffocation, separated from their loved ones in the wild scramble of the night for shelter and safety! Any place, anywhere but there!

Donning our helmets we got to our guns and waited for orders, which we presently received. I never worked with more love and energy than I did that night, and never did I spit more liberally on each individual shell as it was shoved into place for departure. Inside of twenty minutes Fritzie decided that the pastime of shelling Bully-Grenay with gas shells was not as funny as it was cracked up to be; he broke off short and quick.

In the two weeks following we were at Estari Chic, another Vimy Ridge position. Here we were stationed at the horse lines. While there, an order was issued that we could not buy bread from the civilian population for the reason that our military authorities considered the rations we were getting were sufficient for all our needs. The shop-keepers were quite willing to sell any soldier, however, and we were more than anxious to get his bread if we could safely do so. The manner in which we disobeyed orders was as follows: The bake-shop was about half-a-mile from our billet and we had to pass several policemen on the way down; two fellows would stand outside the building while I went inside and purchased the bread, and if policemen were seen coming, the man nearest to the officer would give the signal and I would duck off into an alley-way and up the back streets into the billet, and it would not be long before my outpost would join me; then the jam would be produced and in short order the delicious French bread and jam would be winding its way down into our voracious stomachs.

We left this point for Camblain-le-Abbeau for another nip at the ridge from that angle, pulled into the wagon lines for two days and then got into action on the Lens-Arras road. We laid the guns on the side of the road, camouflaging them in the usual fashion. We were the first battalion to arrive, but within four days 100 or more batteries were there. Our work here was to cut the wire in preparation for one of the usual raids, to blind Fritz and keep him guessing where the drive was to be launched. We performed our work flawlessly, the boys of the infantry going over through the gaps we had made and capturing several machine guns and prisoners.

On the second day following, the Captain asked me to go into the trenches to assist him in observation work. We found after inspection that the point we wanted to get our data upon could not be obtained from the low-lying trenches, and the Captain, wondering where we had best go, happened to get his fancy settled on a mine shaft. "We will go up there, Grant," he said, and together we made our way to the spot. The climb to the top was no easy matter, and when we got there we set about making ourselves as comfortable as possible. As soon as we had our apparatus working, the Captain commenced registering the cemetery, the tombstones of which were being carried away by Fritz to place around his dugouts. The Captain flashed the necessary information and in ten minutes they were pretty thoroughly shot up.

The Captain then directed his attention to a trench digging party, sent his compliments to the guns — would they kindly take care of the trench digging party, which they did. Then we were spotted; in a few seconds we were the recipients of a blast of machine-gun fire; a

S.O.S. Stand to!

minenwerfer dropped at the foot of the mine shaft, blowing the entire corner away, and it became very evident the place was ours no longer, and we started for the bottom.

In going down it was necessary for me to execute a sort of slide, as I had to hang on with my hands while my feet were going down, and the Captain, in his naturally human haste to get to a place of safety, inadvertently trod on my fingers.

"For God's sake, Captain," I yelled, "get off my fingers!"

"Take your damned fingers out of my way!" replied the Captain.

"How can I? Your foot is on them!" He eased up a bit and I was able to release my mangled fingers, but Lord! he weighed about 200 pounds.

Now Captain Black was a man who was absolutely afraid of nothing in human shape; his fighting spirit is unbeatable; every man in the battery can testify to his absolute fearlessness, and I am glad to lend my humble testament to his unquestionable bravery. However, in going down the shaft the shots were coming thick and fast, and it was the most natural thing in the world for him to tread on my fingers in his desire to avoid the sniping shell or machine-gun bullet, but my fingers were sadly in need of repair by the time we got to the bottom.

When we reached the foot we got into the shell hole blasted out by the *minenwerfer* that had torn the corner of the shaft away. We had not yet completed our observations and Cap decided he would try the top of the slag heap. To the top we crawled, placing our periscope and telephone in position, and were nicely settled and doing good work, the Captain congratulating himself audibly on his bright thought in selecting this spot, when his congratulations were cut short by a shell smashing the periscope glass, followed by a *minenwerfer* striking the bottom of the slag heap, making another huge excavation and causing the slag at the top to roll down from under us, taking us with it. But the Cap was not to be driven away so easily. "Come on, Grant, let's try it again," and up we went again, and again another large shell at the bottom of the pile caused a cave-

S.O.S. Stand to!

in, and down we rolled. Still the Captain had not enough, and up we went a third time. The same thing happened again, the shells tearing away a large hole at the bottom of the slag heap, causing the slag on which we were standing to give way and carrying us to the bottom. By this time the shells were showering the entire place and Captain Black reluctantly decided that it was no go, and we gave it up.

It was during the stay of my battery on the Lens-Arras road, during the Vimy Ridge preparation, that I again personally encountered Fritz in the form of his spy system. One night after the guns had been oiled and prepared for their next job, and we were all busy cleaning up the ammunition for the work in hand, I was accosted by a couple of British officers, a Captain and a Major.

"Sergeant, would you kindly help us to a drink of water?" said the Major. "Certainly, sir," I answered, saluting; "if you will wait here a moment I will get it for you."

"Thank you," they replied, and I went for the water. Returning I found the Major with one of our shells in his hand and the Captain examining the gun.

"She's a beauty, Sergeant," said the Captain.

"Yes, sir," I smilingly answered, "and she is just as good as she is beautiful,—never kicks or falters."

"By Jove!" laughed the Major, "that's a good one. How many messages did you send them last night, Sergeant?"

"None, sir."

"You don't say! Why I thought I heard you firing. Where is your battery operating?"

"Oh, we just sent off a few rounds at the crossroads."

"She seems to have been doing her bit today all right."

While conversing with the Major, I noticed the Captain talking with one of my men about the gun sight and, hastily excusing myself to the Major, I went over to him. "Pardon me for interrupting. Billy,

S.O.S. Stand to!

you had better go over to the Major and tell him the gun is ready at once for inspection."

Billy excused himself to the Captain and started off. The officers then prepared to leave.

"Won't you wait a moment, sir, and see the Major? He will be right over."

"Well, we will see him on our way back. We're in a kind of a hurry, Sergeant." And they bade me good night and left.

There was something told me that all was not well with these men, but the suspicion had not become sufficiently rooted in my head to find expression, and, consequently, I said nothing at the time.

The very next morning after inspection, orders were read and in the instructions were explicit descriptions of two British officers who were German agents and who were making the rounds of the lines, picking up information wherever they could, and commanding all ranks to be on the lookout and arrest them on sight, shooting them if they resisted, and offering a prize of ten pounds to the man who succeeded in effecting their arrest. "Good Lord!" I thought. "What a miss!" If my wits had been properly working, I would have been ten pounds the richer, together with a four-weeks' leave of absence.

These audacious agents had visited all sections and doubtless had acquired a store of general information, and headquarters urged a most rigorous search for them. The following night they were spotted in a French *estaminet*, by a bunch of sharp-eyed Tommies, and, as luck would have it, the men were chatting about the ten-pound prize for capturing these same fellows, and their mouths were watering at the picture that each one of them was painting of what he would do if he only had the prize.

"I'll tell 'e what it is," said one, "if my blinkers falls on them chaps I'll wet the whole damned outfit!"

As they entered, the soldier's eye went over the room and lit on the very men in question, seated by themselves in a little side room of the inn. In a low tone he communicated his thought to his

S.O.S. Stand to!

companions. "Blime me, I'll eat your mother-in-law if there ain't our meat!" There was about 20 in the bunch, and they did not waste time in consultation. At once they were in the anteroom, confronting these men.

"What do you want?" gruffly asked the Major.

"We have to come to tell you, sir, that the O.C. wants to see you and the Captain at once."

"All right, tell your O.C. we will be over directly."

"'E wants you now, sir."

"Well, didn't you hear me say we'd be over there shortly?"

"Yes, sir."

"Well, damn you, tell him so, and I'll see that you are taken care of for your impertinence."

"I don't mean to be impertinent, sir, but I'm here to see that you come and come now."

Like a flash both men drew their revolvers, but before they had a chance to use them, the entire bunch was on top of them, and it was a somewhat mussed up Major and Captain that appeared before the O.C. at the headquarters of the Tommies who sleuthed them. The intuition of the soldier proved correct; with absolute certainty he had falconed his prey and the prize was his.

And he was as good as his word. What that bunch didn't have to eat and drink while the money lasted wasn't purchaseable at the front.

S.O.S. Stand to!

CHAPTER XVII
VIMY

With Vimy Ridge in the possession of the Germans, their access for observation placed us at a decided disadvantage; the Lens-Arras, the Mont St. Eloi road—all vital feeding routes for our system—were absolutely open to his inspection at all hours of the day or night; there was no movement along these channels of communication of either men, guns, ammunition, supplies of any kind, of which they were not fully cognizant. So it will be seen that the possession of this elevation was of wonderful advantage to the side holding it.

One of the chief gains to be derived from its possession was the control of the vast coal mines of Lens, one of the richest coal producing sections in France, and the benefit of which has been in German hands since the gray rush first went through. And the possession of the output of these mines gave Fritz a priceless advantage over us. His overlooking position also made it impossible for us to work in the daytime the few coal mines that we had; neither could we supply our guns with the necessary ammunition during the hours of daylight; and further, the possession of this vantage point would release for duty elsewhere a tremendous number of men whose presence there was unavoidable, because of the control he had over the valley and the surrounding country. So, when the chief command decided to take the ridge, they went about the job in a manner thoroughly characteristic of the Scotch commander, Sir Douglas Haig, and his thoroughness was well borne out by the results.

For the space of a month prior to the drive, every hour of the darkness was used to get guns, ammunition and supplies into place; all night long the traffic on the roads was so congested that going faster than a walk with any conveyance, over any part of the channels of communication, was simply out of the question; but when day broke it was imperative that not a single conveyance of any kind be in sight on any road.

S.O.S. Stand to!

Do not imagine, however, that we were free to work as long as the shelter of night lasted; in the artificial light furnished by the flares, Fritz did a lot of damage. On one single night during this work of preparation on the Mont St. Eloi road alone, 156 horses were killed; and on all through roads, each night that the stage was being set for the production of the first scene, casualties were had with deadly regularity.

When everything was in place and the curtain ready to be drawn up, 1400 batteries were in a position along the Lens-Arras road and valley, standing wheel to wheel, many of them brought to bear over roads that had been specially constructed for their conveyance, as regular routes were not usable for them and a road one-and-a-half-miles long, made out of three-inch thick planking, was placed ready for use in three days' time, together with a narrow-gauge railroad, for rushing up ammunition and taking back wounded men. This road and narrow-gauge railway took a short cut across the valley and proved a godsend in relieving the congestion on the regular road, and was of inestimable value in achieving our end.

On the 2nd day of April, 1917, stage manager Haig ordered the curtain raised and, with its raising, vengeance was let loose. Gaps 20 to 30 feet wide were blasted in the barbed wire; some of the mine shafts about Lens were flattened and destroyed; Fritzie's supply roads were rained upon with a steady hail of hell night and day, preventing the entrance to his trenches not only of ammunition, but also of food, and prevented the withdrawal of any men from his lines; his ammunition dumps were set ablaze, the fires from them lighting up the whole country-side for miles around. In the air the efficiency of our preparatory work was equally demonstrated. A new type of flier winged his way back and forth over the sausage-fed warriors, and the ability of our birds to hold the line in the Heavens was amply demonstrated, one British airman, on the 28th of March, five days before the battle began, downing three German eagles in quick succession. Spellbound I watched the magnificent work of this flier.

Far up as the eye could reach, six British planes in battle formation, the leader of the squad about three hundred yards in advance, four

S.O.S. Stand to!

others in a row, the sixth three hundred yards in the rear, winged their way. Suddenly, the rear bird shot downward, volplaning and looping the loop with as much abandon as if he were in an exhibition park. I quickly discerned the object of his lightning-like descent. Hovering over our trenches were three German vultures. As he dropped, Fritz volleyed at him with his anti-aircraft mouthpieces, but failed to land. The bird kept on his downward plunge until he reached his objective, and as he dove into the vultures, our anti-aircraft guns, which had been endeavoring to wing the German birds, ceased fire and all eyes were turned heavenward. With bated breath we watched and waited the outcome.

The Fritzies spread out in circle formation, with a view to surrounding it, each a little higher than the other. With a lightning-like swoop the British bird, getting right in front of it and turning sharply, let fly his machine gun in rapid fire, Fritz answering energetically. In less than three minutes' time, a distinct wabbling was noticeable and the British sparrow, seeing that his work there was done, turned his attention to the others. His work was surely done; Fritz continued to wabble and then plunged in a deadly drop until he got to the Lens-Arras road, where he made a desperate attempt to alight on the highway; but he got tangled up in the trees, his wings being smashed and remaining in the branches, the body of the plane shooting down into a deep ditch and embedding itself and its two occupants in the mud. They were dead. A tremendous cheer greeted this victory over the first opponent. The other two airmen followed our bird, volleying at him as they flew. With a quick motion he turned upside down, swooping for the bird on his upper left, and continued to chase and fight him in this position. The other German bird was off to one side, put-put-put-put-ing! for all he was worth, but his bullets were wasted by reason of the upside down position. In a run of another 500 yards the work of our lad was finished, his machine gun having done the trick; and Fritz and his pilot being killed, the machine dashed rudderless to the ground, nose first.

There remained but one. Our bird again got on top, but there was no fight left in Fritz; he scooted for a hundred yards in the direction of home, but was winged while running, part of his left wing dropping

S.O.S. Stand to!

off. The rest was easy; his machine became unmanageable, an explosive bullet smashed into his petrol tank and he dropped in flames.

The entire ceremony of sending the three German chickens to their eternal hen-coop did not take ten minutes. As each bird fell to its death, the entire valley resounded with wild cheering; and when the last foe fell, the cheering wave of sound was followed by a tiger in the shape of a volley from every rifle—in fact, everything that would shoot, except the big guns.

Our bird then executed his stunt of victory, looping the loop several times over Fritzie's trenches, and the spirit of Fritz was amply exemplified by the thousand times ten thousand shots which were leveled at the air king to bring him down. He bore a charmed life; although his plane was perforated with machine-gun bullets, none touched a vital spot.

But, suddenly, from out the clouds swooped a German swallow in a frenzied attack to retrieve the disgrace. He had all the advantage of position, and a great fear filled my heart that our champion might not long enjoy the fruits of his victory. However, when about 400 yards above our bird, our watchful boys at the Archee guns (the anti-aircraft guns, so nicknamed because of their peculiar explosive sound) opened on him, and with the third shot, off flopped his fish tail. He dove in a wabble to the ground and, in his descent, his petrol tank was struck by one of our explosive bullets. When it reached the ground in No Man's Land, it was a mass of flames.

For seven days, every hour of the night and day, the mighty chorus of 1400 batteries rose and swelled unceasingly in a vast concourse of sound.

Promptly at ten minutes past five, on the morning of the seventh day, the word having passed from end to end of the lines, the men were up and over. A mine that had been prepared in the Ridge by our engineers was exploded, the shock rocking every German trench in the valley, killing several thousand men and wounding twice as many more. The first and second lines were taken without any trouble, and over we went into the third. Some opposition was here met, but quickly overcome. The program was repeated until the entire six lines of German trenches were in Canadian hands, and late in the afternoon we were masters of the Ridge.

The personal comfort to the men taking a stroll through the streets of Arras, after the Ridge was in our possession, had to be seen to be appreciated. Heretofore such a thing as a pleasure walk or shopping tour was out of the question, as the sniping was continuous, and the only way now for Fritz to snipe the town was with his heavy naval pieces, six or seven miles off, and as these visitors are a hundred times scarcer than the callers from the short range boys, the peace and quiet of our fellows were correspondingly increased one hundred fold.

No need now was there to hide our work in and around the coal mines, the precious element being taken out of the bowels of bountiful nature in as large abundance as was required; our hungry guns can now be supplied with all the grub they require in any hour of the twenty-four; our wagon lines moved forward behind the Ridge to a place of perfect security; several army corps were released for service in other parts of the lines, and the city of Lens, honeycombed with German soldiers, is practically bottled up, they not daring to retreat, and it being impossible for them to advance. But the over-weaning advantage of this movement and the reduction of this obstacle is the tremendous impetus that will be given our forces when the waves of the great drive that is in contemplation sweep the gray-clad hordes of Huns from the land of Sunny France. From a military point of view, it can be stated that our success here was of far-reaching importance.

S.O.S. Stand to!

CHAPTER XVIII
BACK TO GOD'S COUNTRY

I spent the two nights following at the wagon lines, taking a much-needed rest, and after my first night's sleep there I sought out a spot in a grassy nook, as far away from the road and bustle of the lines as I could safely go, and lay at full length on the green sward; I felt as if I wanted to lie there forever, without even exerting myself to think. As the sun was setting, I awoke from my day dream, and my stomach felt the call of the cookhouse.

On the day following, one of my chums, Mulhall and myself were ordered to go to the line, gathering up the horses that were wounded or had fallen out through exhaustion. Our errand of mercy to the dumb animals had to be done on horseback, and, with the roads still under observation, it was dangerous for more than two men to go together.

We corralled several of the poor beasts, and their condition of suffering in many instances smote me with a kind of remorse; I couldn't help feeling that we humans were responsible for the pain and misery of these most useful animals that bounteous nature had put upon earth for our comfort and help. We placed them in the ruins of a barn, made them as comfortable as we could, and left them with a supply of water; for feed they had to wait.

It is with much pleasure that I can commend the splendid work in connection with caring for these wounded and sick horses that is being done at the front by the societies organized for that purpose. The amount of suffering alleviated in this, the noblest animal of all, would be ample justification for the work done; but the economic advantage derived in addition makes the object of the societies most worthy in character. Two of the horses that were only slightly wounded I pulled to the line, and as they were inclined to lie down at every step of the way, the condition of my arms when I reached my destination may be imagined; every nerve and muscle from the shoulder down was aching.

S.O.S. Stand to!

When we got to the line, Fritz was retaliating on the Ridge and a heavy bombardment was in progress; our guns were vigorously answering, and over we ran to the gun pit, getting into the game with both feet. After an hour's hard drubbing, I took occasion to step over and see a man whose friendship I had never ceased to curry—the cook, and I was just swallowing the first mouthful of the fruits of my friendship when my joy was rudely interrupted by an orderly.—"The Major wants to see you, Grant." Over I went, wondering what was up, and ransacking my noodle for some breach of discipline of which I might have been guilty.

"Did you want to see me, sir?"

"Yes, Grant," smiled the Major; two officers were standing by and they beamed on me in a fashion that made me think my future mother-in-law had gone on a long journey. "Listen carefully, Grant," said the Major, as he started to read something. I paid strict attention and I could scarcely believe my ears as the true import of the communication commenced to dawn upon me;—the G.O.C. had granted me a furlough and I was instructed to return to Canada immediately on a three-months' leave of absence. I was walking on air for a few minutes, and it was quite some little time before I could make myself really believe I wasn't dreaming.

I lost no time in bidding my pals good-bye, and when I had convinced them that it was an actual fact, the gun Sergeant said, "Fellows, Grant's going; we'll give him the best we've got; ten rounds of gun fire. Ready! Fire!" and ten ear-drum splitters clove the air. I had no cotton in my ears and the effects of that farewell stayed with me several minutes after I left. I then went to say good-bye to the man whose friendship I had always nursed, my good friend the cook. He urged me to wait while he fixed me up the feed of my life, as he expressed it, and you can understand the state of my feelings when I tell you that I refused his bounty. I never did such a thing in my life!

I turned to go and found myself face to face with the Major. "What the hell are you hanging around here for? Didn't I tell you to beat it to the wagon lines before you got hit? Do you think your horseshoe luck is going to stay with you forever? While you have got your furlough in your hand, beat it!"

I hastened my steps. On the way I passed the burial party who were laying to their last rest the men who had fallen the night before, and as I glanced at the faces of the boys who would never again see their beloved Canadian homes, tears, for the first time in many long months, welled up into my eyes.

I doubled from there to a battery in the rear to say farewell to my cousin Hughie, and while going from pit to pit in his battery, looking for him, the guns were speaking as fast as they could, and retaliation from Germany was blasting its way through the air. Right at this moment the Major's warning was most beautifully exemplified; a splinter struck me in the cheek, flooring me and knocking out two teeth in the upper left jaw. When I recovered my balance, the diligence I exercised in getting away from the scene of activity would have satisfied even the Major; besides, I was doubly anxious that he should not know of my mishap, as he would be bound to twit me unmercifully.

Holding my jaw, I made my way carefully to one of the horses I had brought up, mounted, and kicked the poor brute in the ribs every step of the way back to the wagon line. My feelings of sympathy for the animal were completely submerged in the feeling in my jaw, my haste to get to a dressing station, and home. For fear it would reach the Major's ears, I told the doctor at the dressing station that the horse had kicked me. He washed and dressed it with a bandage, but just before getting to the wagon lines I removed it.

Here I had another hard time convincing the fellows that I was off for home, but when they saw me go to the paymaster and draw 50 francs, they were constrained to believe that there must be something in it, and I was the recipient of hearty congratulations and well wishes. Forty of the francs went for champagne and eats; I felt that this might be the last time I would have the opportunity to enjoy the company of many of them.

S.O.S. Stand to!

I departed next morning in the mess cart, and just before leaving I had another send-off;—the entire wagon lines paraded and gave me a parting cheer. Again the tears!

I arrived at Béthune, boarded a French civilian train and traveled for five hours, reaching a junction point where, in company with a number of wounded men who were able to walk, I boarded a box car.

The train was traveling at a funereal pace and the weather turned sharply cold; neither the wounded nor the well men, with one exception, had any blankets; the exception had seven blankets that he monopolized, refusing to share an inch of them with anyone. Such unparalleled hoggishness and meanness never went unpunished at the front, and I resolved that he would be no exception to the rule. In order to take the chill off ourselves, we jumped off the train every chance we got, gathering up some coal, until we had accumulated enough to make a fair-sized fire, which we kindled on the floor of the car; it was necessary to shove the burning coals here and there over the surface to avoid burning a hole through it. At one point I noticed a horse-car filled with straw bedding for the animals, and the train going here at a snail's pace enabled me to jump off and chuck an armful of the straw into our car; I did this with my friend of the blankets in mind. I threw the damp straw on top of the live coals and in a few minutes or less the car was filled with rank, reeking smoke that fairly made the eyes water. Up jumped the blanket monopolist, rushed to the window for a breath of air, and while inhaling the ozone I chucked his blankets out of the car door. When he returned to his nest, which was a nest no longer, he swore several swears, both large and small, but he was forced to fare like the rest of us,—on the bare boards.

All this time the pain in my jaw was gradually getting worse. A swelling had started and I was feeling a little the worse for wear.

It was morning when we reached Abbeville Station, where we were to wait until night before being able to resume our journey. Here there was a horrible mass of dead horses—about 500 in all—lying in the railroad yards; they had died in the cars on the way back for treatment. It was a fearsome sight.

S.O.S. Stand to!

In an hour or so my face was commencing to throb violently, and I hunted up the nearest dressing station, which was a casualty clearing station, and addressed myself to the nurse.

"What's the matter, Canada?" she asked, looking at my jaw.

"Why, I got hit, nurse."

"I can plainly see that, but what makes it that color? It looks like gangrene! Come in and see the doctor."

He examined me and found there was a piece left sticking there; I would have to be operated on at once, he said, and there was no time lost getting down to business. He extracted a small splinter.

"See that this man is put to bed at once; gangrene has just started."

When I got off the table my face was so bound up in bandages that only my nose and one eye were visible.

"Go to bed, now," said the nurse. "Oh, no, I can't," I said; "I have got to leave at once."

"No, no, you mustn't do anything of the kind; you must go to bed at once and have the closest care for some weeks." She fixed up a cot for me in the station and I went to bed. After lying there for three hours I asked her if I might go up to the station and get my kit, that I had some valuable souvenirs I didn't want to lose, and that I would like to present her with some of them. She let me go, and at the station I saw some box cars going through. Grabbing my kit, I slung myself aboard and reached a station by nightfall, where I got off and waited for the through train, which finally came along. The fellows on board with whom I had become acquainted on the way down, told me the hospital orderly was searching for me high and low.

After another wearisome day aboard those unspeakable box-cars, I reached the base. My jaw, although not throbbing so fiercely, was still painfully troublesome, and I sought out one of the hospitals and had to swallow the unwelcome news that the condition of my face was such that it would be necessary to luxuriate in a hospital bed for a week or ten days, which I did.

S.O.S. Stand to!

The kindness of the nurses was beyond praise, and the efforts for the wounded men left nothing to be desired; there was absolutely every provision for the health and well-being of the men. The wonderful organization of the British Red Cross and its workings in this war will go down through the pages of history as the one spot in the nation's management of the campaign that is absolutely flawless.

At the end of ten days I was permitted to leave the hospital, with the understanding that I would take good care of myself and report daily for dressing. I then went to the Y.M.C.A., making my home there for three or four days, and here, also the treatment accorded me was most praiseworthy; the provision made for the men's recreation will remain a lasting tribute to this most beneficial organization.

I left the boys for England, embarking on board ship at 5:00 o'clock in the evening, leaving about an hour later. On the way over submarines were reported in the channel, but my horseshoe luck was still with me, and I made the tight little isle in safety next morning. I arrived at Southampton the latter part of May. My first errand in England was to report to the O.C. at Camp Shorncliffe. Then I made haste to look up my brother Billy, who was in the hospital 200 miles away. On my way to the camp I happened to meet a pal of Billy's, and was delighted to learn that he was well and out of hospital, fully recovered from his wound in the thigh, and in a few minutes' time we were gripping hands.

I never before realized the large measure of affection in our hearts for each other as I did on that morning. It seemed as if we had both been through the Valley of the Shadow and had been led safely through by an all-wise and bountiful Father.

In due time I embarked at Liverpool, on board the Mistress of the Seas, the S.S. *Olympic*, the largest passenger boat afloat. For three days we lay in the channel, awaiting our escort, four torpedo boat destroyers, and, finally, as the wheel of the mighty leviathan commenced churning the waters, I knew we were really off for home!

In starting, we followed the course mapped out for us by three or four of the little channel pilot boats that threaded their way through

S.O.S. Stand to!

the maize of mines placed in the water there, and by night time we were on the bosom of the Atlantic.

The following day was quiet, nothing happened to interrupt the usual monotony of an ocean voyage, but that night at 9:15 the ship from stem to stern was thrown into a turmoil of excitement by the firing of a gun and the terrifying word—"Submarine!" The boat was darkened, not a light showing, and everyone was rushing from their cabins in a mad state for life belts, utterly ignoring the rigid command not to leave their portholes open and expose the lights of the vessel. It was worse than confusion confounded!

I had been appointed one of provo N.C.O.'s, and my duty was to see that everybody was supplied with a lifebelt, wear it at all times except when going to bed, and then they were ordered to have them at hand in case of emergency. Although some of the people obeyed the instructions to the letter, even going so far as to sleep in them, many others neglected the order.

Some idea of the sense of responsibility on the Captain and his crew can be had when I state that 1400 women and children on board were in his absolute care and keeping. Everything possible was done to calm the frantic people; nothing could convince them that that single shot had sunk the sub. But so indeed it was! The steady nerve and unfailing aim of the gunner had done the trick, and there was no more danger to be feared from that particular snake of the sea. The gunner was an old man-o'-war's man and was completely overwhelmed by the grateful and heartfelt thanks of the passengers, he, in his native modesty, apparently thinking he hadn't done any more than he ought to have done,—which indeed was very true. But if he had missed!

There was only one sad mishap throughout the entire excitement. A woman, losing her head and trying to climb into a lifeboat, before she was ordered to do so, and carrying her baby in her arms at the time, as she was clambering up the rail of the vessel to get into the boat, let her baby slip from her arms into the dark waters below. With a frenzied scream, she seemed as if about to throw herself after her little one, but strong hands caught her and prevented.

S.O.S. Stand to!

In spite of the watchful eyes of the four escorts plowing along at each corner of the vessel, and signaling constantly, never for a moment during the time we were in the submarine zone did the ship cease its zigzagging course, and lookouts were stationed on every point of the boat from which observations could be had.

The trip was made in perfect safety and I arrived in Halifax, Nova Scotia, five and a half days from the time I left Liverpool.

At last I was on the train for home! I commenced to count the minutes on the last lap of my journey, and no blushing young girl, making her début, was any more excited than I was when the iron horse choo-chooed into the station at Ottawa two days later. As fast as a taxi could make the trip without violating the rigors of the law against speeding, I dashed homeward. I had sent no word ahead to my people, as I wanted to give them a complete surprise and I succeeded most admirably, my favorite sister fainting as I entered the door.

Printed in the United States
151924LV00009B/142/P